The Customer Experience Book

The Customer Experience Book

How to design, measure and improve customer experience in your business

Alan Pennington

Harlow, England • London • New York • Boston • San Francisco • Toronto • Sydney
Auckland • Singapore • Hong Kong • Tokyo • Seoul • Taipei • New Delhi
Cape Town • São Paulo • Mexico City • Madrid • Amsterdam • Munich • Paris • Milan

PEARSON EDUCATION LIMITED
Edinburgh Gate
Harlow CM20 2JE
United Kingdom
Tel: +44 (0)1279 623623
Web: www.pearson.com/uk

First published 2016 (print and electronic)

ISBN: 978-1-292-14846-5 (print)
        978-1-292-14847-2 (PDF)
        978-1-292-14848-9 (ePub)

British Library Cataloguing-in-Publication Data
A catalogue record for the print edition is available from the British Library

Library of Congress Cataloging-in-Publication Data
Names: Pennington, Alan (Customer experience consultant), author.
Title: The customer experience book : how to design, measure and improve
    customer experience in your business / Alan Pennington.
Description: Harlow, England ; New York : Pearson Education, 2016. | Includes
    index.
Identifiers: LCCN 2016026463 | ISBN 9781292148465 (pbk.)
Subjects: LCSH: Customer relations. | Customer services.
Classification: LCC HF5415.5 .P456 2016 | DDC 658.8/12--dc23
LC record available at https://lccn.loc.gov/2016026463

ARP impression 98

Cover design by Two Associates
Print edition typeset in ITC Giovanni Std 9.5/13 pts by SPi Global
Printed in Great Britain by Ashford Colour Press Ltd

NOTE THAT ANY PAGE CROSS REFERENCES REFER TO THE PRINT EDITION

Contents

CONTENTS

About the author

Alan is a thought leader in the emerging customer experience discipline. Following a successful corporate career that included work in the public, private and agency worlds, he co-founded a consulting business in 2002 focused on providing practical assistance to companies engaging in the development of their customer experience. From small beginnings the business emerged as one of the leading customer experience consultancies in the world. For over 12 years, Alan had the privilege of working across the world with blue chip companies seeing first-hand what does and doesn't work in terms of the internal ability to successfully deliver consistently on brand experiences.

Since then he has focussed on educating and supporting those engaged in the increasingly important strategic discipline of customer experience development and design - turning marketing brilliance into executional experiential brilliance to underpin the billions invested by companies developing brand expectations.

Acknowledgements

I would like to take the opportunity to thank those who have contributed to the writing of this book. This was a new venture for me as the novice author and quite a learning curve. I have been lucky enough to have Eloise to guide me through this from a publisher and editorial perspective – I could not have done this without you and your firm 'nudges' to keep me on track. My readers were a great way to stay in touch with reality, drawn from a wide variety of roles from journalist to chief financial officer to private equity, your inputs were a constant source of insight and contributed to content in a variety of ways. So thanks to Rod, Kate, Bradley, Jonny and Mac: you know who you are!

To my two collaborators: first, the incredible Martha Rogers Ph.D, who has helped me through her knowledge as a seasoned author as well as contributing to my thinking around trust and customer experience. Second, there is Jonathan Carter, who has added real technical insight into my focus on data – he is that rare hybrid that can connect the deep technology with the real needs of the user. Particular thanks to Valerie Peck and the team from SuiteCX who have kindly allowed me to use some screenshots from their leading-edge customer journey mapping and modelling tool.

Over my years of 'experience' in the world of customer experience I have been both inspired and learned a lot from many people. If you are looking for help in the future look up these people and you won't go far wrong: David Hicks, my long-time business partner; Alvin Jackson, Sarah Hobday, Peter Hocknell and Doug Houston from my Mulberry days; and latterly Kerri Nelson, who is leading the charge to connect customer experience to data and predictive analytics.

Last but not least, my thanks go to the Pennington family who have had to deal with the novice writer's frustrations and the sound of constant keyboard tapping over many months.

Publisher's acknowledgements

We are grateful to the following for permission to reproduce copyright material:

Screenshots on pages 75, 97, 99 and 100 courtesy of SuiteCX; figure on p 142 from Kaplan, R S. and Norton, D. P., 'Using the balanced scorecard as a strategic management system', *Harvard Business Review*, 76, © Harvard Business Publishing 1996.

Photos on p 126 © Kumar Sriskandan/Alamy Stock Image (top) and © ImageBROKER/Alamy Stock Image (bottom).

Contribution on pp. 168–9 courtesy of Jonathan Carter, and on pp.174–84 courtesy of Martha Rogers, Ph.D.

Net Promoter, NPS, and the NPS-related emoticons are registered service marks, and Net Promoter Score and Net Promoter System are service marks, of Bain & Company, Inc., Satmetrix Systems, Inc. and Fred Reichheld.

Introduction

If you are reading this introduction you are one of the growing numbers of individuals engaging with the customer experience, and recognising that customer experience is one of the fastest-growing components of business strategy.

In this book we will look at the cultural, functional and emotional aspects of the customer experience and learn how to deploy some of the growing array of tools and techniques that will improve experiences. It is aimed at the CEO and senior executives who intuitively know that their customer experience is important but have struggled to drive change; it is aimed at the more junior leaders who so often have the passion and inspiration but are frustrated by their organisation's inability or unwillingness to embrace the truth; it is also aimed at the true converts who have and still are driving the customer experience agenda in their businesses and want some further guidance on how to get even better at delivering.

The title for this book reflects the need at this point to provide help and practical guidance on the 'how to' in customer experience terms. As the market and the discipline mature over the next few years the next edition of this book may better reflect the true importance and commercial advantage by being re-titled *Experience – the difference! The Customer Experience Book*.

Today there are few formal programmes and educational guides to turn to as you seek to understand how best to develop and manage the customer experience that your company delivers. In the early 2000s, businesses were recognising that the customer experience would be the 'next business tsunami'. Intuitively most employees from the front line to the boardroom accept that focusing on what your customer needs and delivering against those needs is a 'good thing' to do – yet today all over the world companies are consistently delivering substandard experiences.

In an age where the power of the customer has never been stronger and our experience set against our expectations is increasingly driving the choices we make, why are we not seeing huge improvements?

Why, for example, when a company has spent billions developing a car would they not invest in an experience that complements that investment? Yet the car sales experience has barely changed in 50 years. It would take a fraction of the percentage of the investment in the car to revolutionise the way that we as car buyers experience the brand.

- Why after investing many millions in the creation of a brand and identity would companies leave the experience that customers have largely to chance?
- Why would a company outsource its contact with customers to a third-party call centre and not ensure that the experience at an emotional level is being delivered in a way that meets the expectations created by the brand message.
- Why do most call centre key performance indicators still focus on quantitative measures like call duration, calls abandoned, wait time, etc.?
- Why do boardroom agendas not have customer at the top?
- Why do company executives sitting in the boardroom not know the top five complaints about their experience and operation?
- Why do companies still believe that buying research and investing in customer relationship management (CRM) technology will be the answer to improving their customer experience?

The answers to these and many more questions are covered in this book – but in summary there are some simple answers to the main questions.

Much of the problem is in the stilted thinking that exists, with many experiences not really changing for years – for example, the car buying experience on the forecourt is unchanged from the 1970s. The view that we have always done it this way prevails and companies find it very difficult to 'think differently' – that makes it easy for new entrants like Zappos to star in terms of experience as the existing players are locked into their existing experience.

Equally, where companies do innovate, others see the answer as replication rather than further innovation, and so are constantly playing catch up. Apple changed the game by creating open-plan stores, removing the need for checkouts and overloading the store with staff. None of these changes is that huge, but the biggest decision was to put more people than they may need into the stores – in the scale of Apple the investment is small but remains significant. It does not make perfect financial sense, but it is spot on for the brand and the expectations that it creates. When it was announced in 2012 that staffing would be reduced, the social media firestorm created was enough to influence and create a U-turn: 'Making these changes was a mistake and the changes are being reversed,' an Apple spokesperson said. If we look at Samsung stores today they are seemingly replicating the look of Apple, but not the investment in the staffing.

Customer experience as a discipline is still in its infancy, those charged with improving experience are having to 'make it up as they go along' – few company training activities focus directly on the customer experience, preferring to address the much narrower customer service instead. So what is the difference? Put simply, customer experience embraces the way that a company operates across all functions – it recognises the contribution required from across the company. It addresses the need for companies to accept that their culture needs to evolve to embrace the customer experience agenda and to integrate it into the business strategy.

In the past, customer experience was badged in the marketing and brand category and fell foul of the old marketing adage of being fluffy: '50 per cent of marketing works and 50 per cent doesn't – the problem is we don't know which 50 per cent works.' It was not clear that you could draw a straight line between an investment in experience improvement and the bottom line of the company. Today that is not the case and there are clearly demonstrable lines of sight.

The customer experience world still suffers from the legacy of failed CRM investments, and there were some very large investments in infrastructure that companies later called into question. Some consulting and technology vendors have simply rebadged their old CRM practice as customer experience, but the fundamentals of their thinking and operation have not changed.

People fear the unknown and the consequences of engaging in the customer experience world – how as a senior executive or an employee do I fit this 'additional work' into my already full calendar? What would I actually need to do?

So whether you are the CEO, senior director, customer experience director, customer experience programme lead or a frontline employee, there is
content for you – from simple 'how to' explanations to advice on how to
engage your organisation

For more insights into the world of customer experience visit my blog at
www.thecustomerexperiencebook.com

Hope you enjoy the experience of this book ☺

Part

1

Customer experience in business

1

Does your customer experience happen by design or by accident?

The simple fact is that most companies do not think through the actual experience that they want to deliver at key times and so they do not actively design in that experience.

As you read this page your company is delivering experiences and it is likely that the vast majority will be a reflection of the person delivering them rather than any well-defined and equipped experience deliberately designed to deliver on that massive investment in creating the expectation.

Consider what changes and why your company might decide to focus and invest more heavily in both understanding its customers and designing experiences?

There is a point in time when the need or desire to provide a greater focus on the customer is initiated and a plan is required, so what are the triggers? Here are a few for you; consider whether they apply in your business:

1. The company has a new CEO appointed and that individual believes in the power of the customer.

2. The company has exhausted all other avenues from cost-cutting to marketing-led sales drives.

3. The company is struggling to differentiate itself from the competition in terms of either product/service or price; of course if this is a start-up then differentiation may be the business driver!

In two out of three cases here the start point is a reaction to business problems – and in the case of the new CEO, the business will probably see the statement as a business problem! Starting from a position of negativity is not usually a recipe for success.

Whatever the trigger, however, having the initial impetus to improve the experience has to be seized and taken forward.

It is critical to success in the customer experience environment to start to use the senior team focus to challenge the way that your company interacts with your customers, this chapter brings into focus the need to never accept the status quo or the 'we have always done it this way' and 'it isn't broken so don't fix it' view. It challenges the reasoning behind a failure to change experiences and looks at the huge often missed opportunity of the digital experience development. We will also consider how many companies fail to even think about designing critical interactions, how 'wow' moments are often actually disasters and show how focusing on high-value interactions can have an exponential impact on customer behaviours.

The reality is that experiences often happen because there is an already-accepted solution – we don't challenge the status quo and ask the question 'is that really the best way to do this?'

For example, why is it that you can only get your car serviced or repaired Monday to Friday 9 a.m.–5 p.m. and perhaps Saturday morning? My need as a customer is to have my car serviced when I don't need it, in my case typically that is in the evening and at night and yet convention tells me that this is not possible. Yet from the garage viewpoint would it not make more commercial sense to have an operation working 24/7 sweating the asset that is a workshop and tools that currently lie idle for over 50 per cent of the average day?

The business of actively designing an experience begins with the building of the expectation of what that experience will be. So it is no surprise that the initial stages tend to be owned by the brand and marketing teams. It is their job to create demand pull from the customer and to create an expectation that the product or service is 'worth trying' and should meet a particular need the customer has – this could be as simple as washing detergent that cleans out stains, to a luxury car that underpins the status or lifestyle of the customer.

Every company board sees the need to 'advertise' and while they might not be able to discern for certain which part of that advertising is having the most effect they see the need to continue to invest in a range of activities.

Every business plan around the world now has a marketing and brand line and it is significant – picture a business that did not have a line in their plan: it would, in short, be seen as commercial suicide.

Of course there is always one and in this case it is 'geek squad'. Its founder Robert Stephens built his business through word of mouth, designing a great experience people would talk about. He is quoted as saying that 'advertising is a tax for having an unremarkable experience'.

One of the main reasons why experiences are not designed to better effect is that there is no reflection of the need to invest directly in the customer experience in the annual planning round. Customer experience is not seen as important enough in the strategic and budget planning to be singled out for specific and significant investment. Equally it is not integrated effectively into the wider budget and plan process; if it is you will begin to question some of the investments that you make.

Let's look at some of the big areas of expenditure that most companies will have as line items annually and consider some questions that you should be asking.

Your company will quite rightly recognise that the development of your data and IT capability is going to be key to continued business success. How could you run without the daily need to upgrade and refine that backbone of the delivery? The thirst for more and more data – big data – through which to better manage the customer knows no bounds in terms of spend.

But ask yourself the following: how much do we spend on gathering data and what evidence do we have that it is actually converting into an improved experience? How much do we take on faith and the belief that if a competitor is doing it we must too? And where is the data actually used to actively bring about change or improvements – perhaps 10 per cent is, but which 10 per cent?

Is data being actively used to improve the actual customer experience?

Companies also see value in market research to learn more about their customers, their needs, their beliefs, their wants – indeed there is a real desire to know everything about everyone! How much is invested each year in longitudinal tracking surveys that rely often on outdated questions that have remained static (for tracking purposes) over many years despite huge changes to customer needs and perceptions?

Remember before you commission research in the customer experience space ask yourself 'how will I actually use what I find out to deliver positive improvements or change?'

Your customers' needs and expectations are constantly changing: how are you keeping up to speed with those current, real-time needs?

These investments are ticked through in the annual spending round because they are 'part of the furniture', yet companies need to think differently today about how they engage with their customers.

Ask yourself these questions:

- Who in your company uses long-term tracking research findings?
- What has changed as a result of these huge investments?
- Would we miss it or what would be different if we stopped them?

All too often market research findings are little more than a comfort blanket for the executive team who can sit comfortably in the boardroom reviewing the annual survey that says their customers are satisfied or very satisfied. Research companies have grown off the back of embedded surveys over the years but they do not get real access to boardrooms and are unable to underline the value they have provided by connecting this to customer experience change. This space is now being similarly attacked by data businesses claiming to be able to predict our very behaviours based on complex algorithms – in fact, huge investment is being made to achieve this Holy Grail.

You only have to look at some of the spectacular business failures to learn that 'believing the research' can be a dangerous friend in the boardroom as it breeds complacency and inactivity – we only say we are very satisfied until someone presents us with a better option: then we are off!

Remember that most research is retrospective and it can be too late by the time you have collated what is deemed to be enough evidence of the need to change

Worse still, market research is used to kill ideas before they ever get off the ground.

How many times do you ignore your intuition and business sense and instead challenge a team to go away and research a sample of people to consider if it might be a good idea?

The other big area of spend is process engineering or business process re-engineering, which consumes vast resources in businesses and is focused largely on the industrial view of the world and its drive for efficiency and cost reduction. This has over the years spawned a plethora of methodologies from Six Sigma to Kaizen and there are today millions of people working in this discipline.

Their success is typically measured through efficiency and reduced cost to serve or produce – rarely is it measured in terms of the resulting customer experience, or at best where there is a customer experience measure it is seen as a lower order of importance.

The efforts in this space are almost always internally driven and focus on what is best for the company, not the customer. As a simple example, a bank reviewed its call centre 'process' and decided to eliminate 10 seconds from a call in order to reduce costs – by multiplying 10 seconds by thousands of calls a simple case is made. The reduction meant that the agent no longer said at the end of a call, 'Is there anything else I can help you with today?' In experiential terms this is an important and positive way to close off a call, but in a lean process environment an opportunity to reduce a cycle time.

To put this into clearer focus:

- eMarketer in 2015 estimated that global spend on brand marketing (to create the expectation) was **US$592 billion**.
- Gartner's *Market Databook, 3Q15 Update* estimated **US$4 trillion** spend on IT in 2015.
- ESOMAR's *Global Market Research* report for 2014 shows world research turnover rose 0.1 per cent in 2014 to **US$43 billion**!
- There are no figures for business process reengineering (BPR), but we can assume it will be very significant.

What was the investment in ensuring that the US$592 billion spent on creating an expectation was realised in terms of the actual experience that we as customers enjoyed?

Again no figures exist today, but we can safely be assured that investment directly into the design, management and measurement of the customer experience was a fraction of a fraction of a percentage point of that spent on creating those expectations.

On the upside, the reality is that not every experience needs a fully executed experience design, but there are critical points in any company's interactions with the customer where there is a higher than normal risk of that experience impacting customer behaviours and opinions, and therefore actions.

Failure to take control of these critical interactions and ensure that an experience is both deliberately designed and then staff trained and equipped to deliver it consistently, is a significant business risk.

The customer experience challenge

The challenge is to understand where the inflection points are; that is, where the customer has a high expectation and emotional engagement and the business fails to meet those expectations during the customer journey. This is an easy way to provide early definition of where to make the major investment in the active design of the experience.

The reality is that not all interactions are equal in terms of their impact on us as customers; intuitively we all understand that to be the case, but how do you highlight the critical interactions in your particular business. This is at the heart of the return on investment from work in the customer experience discipline – being able to directly connect activity that relates to the customer experience and the behaviours and actions of customers that impact on the bottom line of the company. This can be an impact on either side of the balance sheet, from reducing cost to serve, to increasing spend or share of wallet.

The production of an outside-in customer journey map (CJM), tracking and collating all of the interactions a customer has during an experience from the customer's viewpoint, is one positive step to gaining an understanding of the customer view beyond simple company-led research. We discuss how to create a CJM in detail in Chapter 6.

The end-to-end view that an external-focused CJM provides also reveals fault lines in the way that different functions in the company define what 'to be a customer' actually means and how the way they are measured drives their specific understanding and behaviours to the detriment of the business.

For example, a detailed CJM in the financial services credit card business reveals that the definition of a 'customer' varies widely between different departments, and this also means their success rates are skewed as well.

- The department/provider responsible for adding prospects into the system views a customer as a 'lead generated' regardless of whether they apply for the credit card or not.
- The team that vets the application and issues the plastic considers a customer as being the person who has received their plastic within the set time limit, whether they use the card or not.
- The team that handles card activation views someone as a customer once they have successfully activated the card – yet if

that customer fails to transact or has the card 'at the back of the wallet' not as their primary card, then from a business perspective they are never really customers.

Despite a series of green lights at individual levels, and indeed payments being made for success, they are just an unrecovered cost.

Given these varying definitions between departments, it's clear to see that in terms of the customer journey, the teams are never going to be aligned.

Aligning these different definitions and providing a common measurement across functions is a simple way to begin to provide a common understanding of what a customer truly is – so in this case no one gets a green light or payment until a prospect has become an active and trading primary customer.

Remember that what gets measured gets done – look at how different owners of the customer experience are measured and align measures across teams

You do have easily accessible information and data locked away inside the company that can help to highlight the inflections and pinpoint where the customer value is being created and destroyed within the CJM.

What are your top five customer complaints: which part of the journey do they refer to?

We as customers tend to expend our energy complaining because it really matters emotionally. Where is the company getting positive feedback from customers, and what is it that you are doing that is causing that to happen. At its simplest, consistently good experiences are about fixing the problems and doing more of what you are doing well. If the positive feedback relates to a specific individual, what are they doing that others are not – can you raise the profile of that individual, can you export an approach or an idea they have had?

Using 'moments of truth' and 'pain points'

The convention for defining these key interactions and inflection points is to talk about 'moments of truth' and 'pain points', and quite often these two collide at a particular point where the experience is both important and painful, which presents an opportunity for a double-win. This provides a simple way of deciding how to prioritise activity as it offers a win–win for both the company and the customer.

My preferred way to look at both of these is to consider the level of emotional investment being made by the customer, and it is usually true that both moments of truth and pain points are points at which we as customers are more emotionally invested than at other times.

For example, in the insurance world when you have an accident or your roof leaks you are in a significantly enhanced emotional state and therefore much more likely to remember 'how someone made you feel' at that point. It is at that point that the expectation and indeed the customer promise that has been made in the brand advertising crystallises one way or the other.

So in the case of an insurer who used the line 'we won't make a drama out of a crisis', what happened when that call is made is the defining moment in the relationship. If that conversation begins with 'hello, what is your policy number?' rather than 'hello, firstly can I check are you ok, now if you can give me your full name I will find your policy details' the customer reaction is going to be different. The cost to the company of the difference in the opening words is zero but the impact on the customer is huge. The true impact of the experience is felt at the point of renewal where the customer votes with their feet about how they felt.

Remember you need to consider all of the senses in customer experience – language is cheap to change and powerful as a part of the experience design

The experience at an ATM needs to be functional and intuitive: the interface needs to be clear and easy to use and it needs to deliver the simple transaction. However, the act of a face-to-face opening of a bank account is much more complex and is a critical point in the relationship between customer and bank. Persuaded by the advertising and perhaps friends' recommendations, a significant investment is being made by the customer – yet even after opening the account it may then remain 'dormant' as the customer fails to activate it as a consequence of how they felt during the 'opening experience'. This is the perfect opportunity to design an experience in detail and ensure that the members of staff delivering that experience are both trained and equipped to ensure that the experience not only matches but also exceeds the expectation. This means not only the 'process' but also the environment: from seating to lighting, the smells, sights and sounds, understanding the emotional state of the customer, and responding to both spoken and unspoken needs. Investing at this point has the potential to create a significant lifetime value benefit. We will look at this in more detail when we consider how to set about actively designing an experience in your company.

Remember a customer is not a customer until they are actually doing business with you consistently and have accessed all the benefits that are available to them

The internal pain point is not having a specific line in the business plan for customer experience. Any spending that is undertaken tends to be 'project related' and therefore discretionary, having to be begged for and easily cut in times of adversity.

Remember you need to insert the customer experience design into the annual planning process

Can we really design in 'wow' experiences and do we want to?

When it comes to customer experience we often see companies trumpet a story about an employee who has gone the extra mile, and we all have our anecdotes about how someone has done something extraordinary to help out a customer. The problem with these so-called 'wow' experiences is that behind them there is usually a failure. It is the heroic efforts of an individual that saves the day and becomes newsworthy. On the positive side, that can show the business culture in a positive light – do what you need to aid the customer, use your initiative. But of course the real challenge is to avoid the need for the heroic recovery in the first place.

However, it would make little commercial sense for a company to deliver these 'wow' moments every day; indeed they would soon no longer be 'wow' moments but the norm, raising the bar on everyday expectations.

Your challenge is to create a consistently good experience that meets the expectation created by your brand and to know where it is possible to exceed those expectations at a critical moment.

To illustrate this, consider the following scenario. A small, bespoke travel company puts a bottle of wine and handwritten note in their returning customers room as a unique and private welcome. As the business begins to grow, a smart marketer put this into the brochure. Now, what was a 'wow' moment becomes an expectation that can then lead to complaints if the wine does not appear or the note is not delivered!

Remember that 'wow' moments are the exception. Truly great experiences are about consistency over time

While taking the learning from the travel company and not industrialising the 'wow', it is possible for a company to actively design in a 'wow' moment that has specific impact at a specific moment in time.

To illustrate what I mean, I designed an experience for an estate agent (or realtor in the USA) around the moment when a buyer takes possession of their new property. Bearing in mind that this is most likely the biggest single capital outlay an individual ever makes and that it may be some time before they are going to be a customer again, the challenge was to leave a lasting positive memory without taking over the positive memories of the day. The solution showcases my mantra that small pieces of data used to great effect are far more powerful than cyber warehouses of data that are never used and cost you to store!

So picture the scene: the agent is showing a couple around a potential property, they move into the garden where the agent talks about the space and casually asks, 'Do you enjoy gardening, what flowers do you like? Personally I love geraniums.' The couple reply 'white roses', and the conversation moves on. The agent returns to the office and makes a note of the answer, one single piece of data. If and when the customer finally buys a property the agent then arranges for a vase of fresh white roses to be on the kitchen surface ready for when they walk in. The flowers alone are a nice gesture; the magic is that they are their favourite flowers – that creates the mini 'wow' which even if not noticed consciously will have been noticed sub-consciously in the melee of the day.

Remember we are in the memories business in customer experience and this is about designing for positive ones; attention to detail is critical to success

It is the cumulative impact of small changes that creates an improved experience and contributes to an evolution of the customer culture. Small things equal BIG IMPACT

The digital experience challenge

The rise of digital has added another layer of complexity to the customer experience – some experiences are now entirely digital, while through a customer lens a growing number are now expected to be seamless across channels. The ability to create an amazing online experience can often be at odds with the switch to the physical experience. For example, the huge growth in home shopping has created a whole new need for a delivery experience to match that online experience. As Amazon experiments with 'drone deliveries', the appetite for immediacy available online is seeing the development of same-day deliveries and Sunday deliveries being seen as the new benchmark. Equally the volume of home deliveries is creating a whole new market outside the accepted channels of postal service, and major logistics companies. Small-scale local operators and hubs based out of your garage add both experience improvements and risks in equal measure. The web site experience is analogous with brand advertising in the sense that it can easily create an expectation of service and experience which is not replicated once the channel switches to call centre, traditional bricks and mortar location or a physical delivery happens.

Remember that from the customer perspective, experiences are seamless and there is an expectation of consistency across channels – but different internal owners of parts of that experience cause inconsistency. You must take a longitudinal view of the total experience to spot inconsistency

Even car buying is now a multi-channel experience, with much of the purchase decision being researched and made online before the customer switches channel and goes to the physical showroom. At that point the customer has knowledge and expects the salesperson to have at least as much and more knowledge than they do – all too often the showroom fails that basic test, the power moves to the customer and respect for the brand is impacted.

The irony of customer experience is that your end customer typically has a better view of your experience than your company as they are exposed to the end-to-end experience not just parts of it.

Organisationally, companies have responded by setting up specific 'digital' teams that work in that environment and optimise for their world – in effect they have added another level of inconsistency to the customer experience. It is critical that any online experience expectations are commensurate with the other channels that a customer will touch as part of their overall interactions with the company. The customer has the advantage of seeing the various parts of your business, while the individual internal teams typically just seek to optimise their component and are not exposed to the upstream and downstream components.

Remember in customer experience terms you are only as good as your weakest link – sometimes you need to slow down development in one channel to provide a consistent and not jarring experience

Things to think about

In summary, the customer experience discipline is still emerging from the shadows, but it is beyond question the case that your business cannot leave the delivery of your critical experiences to chance. That means that understanding what matters to customers, actively designing critical experiences, equipping teams to deliver on that design and connecting the customer outcomes to the bottom line are now business essentials. Every company should have a line in the annual plan to cover the active development and management of their customer experience. This does not even need to be incremental: as a start point you should consider investing a mere 10 per cent of the brand and advertising budget directly into the delivery of an experience that matches the expectation – that makes perfect sense.

2

Connecting with your customer to create a customer intelligent company

To understand the future you need to understand the past and this chapter looks at some of the reasons why companies still find engaging in meaningful customer-based activity very hard to accommodate. We will explore:

- Why you should move your thinking from being a customer-centric company to being a more customer intelligent company?

- What is the impact of the inequity of investment in infrastructure and the actual delivery of a customer experience? In the theatrical world this is like investing in a set but not in the script, story or actors.

- What is the legacy of the 1980s/90s investments in CRM systems and the relative lack of understanding about how to embrace the customer from an organisational design perspective?

Let's explore the notion of the 'customer intelligent' company and consider how to give practical guidance to those serious about wanting to turn their intuitive belief into real programmes and then to make being customer intelligent an integral part of their business DNA *not* because it is fashionable or because it feels good to be 'nice' to customers, but because it makes sense from a company, an employee and their customers' point of view. Happy employees stay longer, work harder and attract people like them to join your company, while customers spend more, stay longer and advocate your company more. Many executives see this as a 'new journey' and one that will require them to become customer centric and incur significant investments both in terms of cash and other resources – it is this fear that dilutes the enthusiasm and the eventual level of deployment of customer-based strategies.

Put simply companies and executives are wrong.

The customer intelligent company uses all of its knowledge and connects the customer into the very heart of its operation and decision making – the customer intelligent company has a very high level of self-awareness of its position in its customers' lives and is in tune with the rhythm of their lives.

We have all heard companies claim that they either are or intend to become customer centric but what does that really mean and how realistic is that?

According to Investopedia, customer centricity is a 'specific approach to doing business that focuses on the customer. Customer/client centric businesses ensure that the customer is at the centre of a business philosophy, operations or ideas. These businesses believe that their customers/clients are the only reason they exist and use every means at their disposal to keep the customer/client happy and satisfied.'

If we accept those words it means that the customer agenda will be at the centre of company thinking and dominant in the company, driving both strategic choices and day-to-day actions.

How many examples can you think of where that goal has been achieved when applied to an already-established business?

I struggle to name any because it is an unrealistic goal and involves such a cultural and strategic shift that it is easily suppressed through the passive aggressive actions of individuals across the organisation. So why not avoid this unachievable ambition and instead seek to be *more* customer intelligent instead?

A customer intelligent company will be both more efficient in terms of its operation and more effective at translating the often huge spend on marketing and product development into bottom line profitability.

Think about your own life and instances where you have seen a great advert and then when you tried the product or service it failed to live up to the expectation that had been created in your mind. You end up more disappointed than if you had never even tried it. Or think about a product that has clearly had a lot of development money spent on it – but the wrapper of the human experience does not reach the standard set by the product. We can all do this and it means that the investments made in advertising our product are not fully crystallised for the end customer.

Compare that with the Apple iPad that has managed to bridge the gap between technology and experience to the extent that my children credited it with emotions. What do I mean? When about to go on holiday a few years ago the children asked the question 'Is iPad coming with us?' An innocent phrase, but consider the phrasing of the question and you see that it meant they saw the iPad in the same terms as perhaps a dog, something to be considered, so we ended up taking another 'family member' along with us to Spain!

What are the characteristics of a customer intelligent company?

Ask yourself the following questions and see where you can honestly say, 'yes we do that':

- A customer intelligent company understands the cost of failure in terms of its customer promise, for example how much time and budget you spend resolving what are often self-inflicted customer problems.

- A customer intelligent company's staff all know what experience they are required to deliver.

- A customer intelligent company understands the precise points in the customer journey where value is either created or destroyed.

- A customer intelligent company uses customer needs to actively design the critical interactions with customers.

- A customer intelligent company monitors a range of key customer-outcome-driven measures and makes changes based on those results.

- A customer intelligent company ensures all employees understand how their actions impact on the customer, including both frontline and back office teams.
- A customer intelligent company spends enough time and resources to train staff to deliver on the customer/brand promise.
- A customer intelligent company is making small course adjustments every day to improve the experience.

In short, a customer intelligent company understands the value of connecting with a customer's mind as well as their wallet and that to do the former you will improve your results in terms of the latter.

The concept of customer intelligence is nothing to be scared of, it is not a rebadging of CRM (customer relationship management), it is not about an IT solution (and all the financial pain that brought) – it is about using the wide range of information already available and using that information more intelligently to better inform how to deliver and what to deliver through the customer experience. I will argue later that, in fact, customer experience is not about 'big data', it is about 'little data', it is not about big spend it is about small spend – it is about using what already exists to become more customer intelligent. That will mean centralising information that relates to your customer experience and connecting different teams and departments that own parts of the experience today. It will also mean thinking differently about the business and how you design experiences. To be intelligent you need to be able to view customer experiences from the outside in, and identify and understand the critical stages in a life cycle of experience so that you actually invest where you can make a difference. Successful customer experiences are part science and part art: it is all about mindset and culture, and it is this blend that creates success.

Remember 95 per cent of what you need to improve your customer experience will already exist in the company. The role of the customer

experience team is to act as the catalyst, the connector and facilitator inside the company

The continuing debate over the value of investing in the customer experience has acted as a brake on its development as a discipline. It has taken several years to build sufficient evidence to convince boardroom sceptics, but the evidence to support the link between commercial and stock market success and the delivery of a superior customer experience continues to grow every year. The latest round of studies has reinforced this view showing that where the customer experience is rated high the stock performance is similarly high, and vice versa.

Studies in both the United Kingdom and USA bring this correlation into stark context – what is significant is that both studies now have trends over many years that are consistent.

The UK customer experience top 100 achieved double the five-year revenue growth of the FTSE 100.

Customer experience excellence top 100 growth by sector compared to FTSE 100 from 2012–2015

	FTSE 100	CEE Top 100
Financial Services	+5.4 per cent	+14.2 per cent
Travel & Hotels	+3.7 per cent	+5.1 per cent
Non-Grocery Retail	+6.5 per cent	+15.8 per cent
Grocery Retail	+0.2 per cent	+5.7 per cent

Source: KPMG-Nunwood CEEC 2015 UK Analysis

What we see across the globe is that it is increasingly the case that product offerings are closer to parity and more easily imitated, which means that creating and managing a positive and memorable customer experience is often your single greatest source of sustainable differentiation and therefore competitive advantage. The good news is that customers are prepared to pay for a better service experience. As far back as 2012, Oracle's research report 'Why Customer "Satisfaction" is No Longer Good Enough' revealed that, 81 per cent of customers surveyed are willing to pay more for superior customer experience. With nearly half (44 per cent) willing to pay a premium of more than 5 per cent.' In the UK Institute of Customer Service survey February 2014, 25 per cent confirmed they would prefer a higher level of service and 'were prepared to pay a premium for it'.

Remember the evidence is that your customers will pay more for a better experience and delivering a poor experience will cost you more. By improving the delivery of your experience you will be impacting positively on both sides of the balance sheet

Post the financial crisis of 2008 many companies implemented wholesale cuts to their business operations, often with little knowledge of the impact on their customer's experience. We now know that it is important to understand your customers and what they really value about their interactions with you and as a result boardrooms have started to take the value of experience seriously. This has opened the door to us as customer experience practitioners to really push the agenda.

Remember we can thank the financial crisis that has caused business leaders to go back to the business basics, without customers you have no business! Today's connected world is allowing start-ups to disrupt the established companies by focusing on experience

We know that understanding how to gain and keep customers over time is increasingly critical at a time when customers have more and more choice, not only in terms of product but also channel and the experience they are prepared to pay for. Understanding what a customer values in terms of the experience and what are the critical interactions that drive their behaviours and then actions is at the heart of customer experience. The rise of the small business designed to exploit the best market opportunities is another key market factor – they feed off the mistrust of the incumbent who is seen to have underdelivered or exploited their market position in experiential terms.

If you think about your business, how easy it is to match product changes quite quickly, but if you think about copying a brand reputation around best-in-class experience that is much harder and intangible. That translates into a much more sustainable advantage and as has been evidenced has significant extra benefits.

When you are recognised for your customer experience:

- you are often seen as innovators;
- your stock performance is likely to be better than your competitors;
- you will enjoy lower staff churn rates, which means you get to keep your best performers longer and avoid the cost in cash and quality of replacing key leaders;
- the cost of handling complaints falls;
- the company benefits from the free positive customer word of mouth and the associated 'halo effect';
- your customers are more willing to share ideas and improvements;
- your customers will bank a higher level of 'forgiveness' when you make a mistake.

Put simply, your customers would rather you existed than not – can you claim that about your company?

Preparing to connect with your customers

If you ask yourself which companies you admire, most people will end up thinking about brands that have great products but they are complemented by great and differentiated experiences. In many cases they will not even have experienced the product or service themselves but they have heard positive messages, the 'halo effect' – today's customers talk about their great experiences and their terrible experiences with equal passion.

Remember brands that we admire are typically those that deliver consistently and occasionally exceed our expectations

If the case both intuitively and empirically is so strong the question has to be why are more companies not fully engaged with delivering on this key part of a business strategy?

It has become clear over a number of years that the easiest way to lose traction inside a business is to always tag the word customer to a subject. Why is this? By tagging the word customer it is possible to switch off a significant portion of an organisation's management and staff who immediately assume that the ownership must lie with either marketing or customer service – after all, they are the only people who really have customers, right? Even sales teams often only have customers when they need them to complete a sale or affect a renewal; there was an old retail adage that said, 'life would be just great if it wasn't for customers'. Of course the reality is that everyone in a company has an impact on the end customer, they just don't see it and nobody helps them to make the connections that are required in order to do so.

Back in 2004 in their book *Building Great Customer Experiences* Colin Shaw and John Ivens talked about their view that 'the customer experience will be the next business tsunami'. The problem is that few companies actually had approaches in place to deal with that 'business tsunami' effectively, and the same remains true today as leaders struggle to come to terms with what they actually can do in practical terms to drive business benefit from this knowledge.

Your question is how well prepared and capable are you today in terms of the day-to-day practicality of what can be done today, tomorrow and the next day to address it? As ever in these situations your company will probably see itself as unique and your industry or sector as unique too, requiring bespoke solutions when the reality from many engagements is that the Pareto principle is not far out in terms of the 80 per cent of issues and solutions that are cross sector, geography and industry. It is usually just a matter of degrees of influence of specific factors that weigh more heavily in one area or another.

For example, bringing new customers on board is a very common issue for companies whether they are business-to-business or business-to-consumer – for a bank it may be more important than an online retailer, but it is important to both nonetheless. The 20 per cent may require some specific work, but if the companies could get to the 80 per cent first then the 20 per cent would follow later. What I have found over time is that the focus tends to be on the difficulties while the basics – less 'sexy' but absolutely fundamental and often where the early wins are to be found – are not addressed.

Remember all companies have one thing in common – people are customers who want a product, a service or probably both

What else can we say has held back the progress of customer experience? Well not least the fact that it is not considered a discipline in the same field as perhaps areas such as finance, marketing, sales and business process re-engineering. The whole area has tended to be classified as 'soft'. In some senses those of us engaged in the world of customer experience did it a disservice by not more strongly developing the financial links between the customer experience and business performance, this gap is now being filled quickly as more and more tracking-based evidence is emerging from respected sources including Forrester Research.

The make-up of the top executives across sectors has had an impact with a significant proportion drawn from the world of finance – these individuals while interested in the concept have almost to act against their likely personal profiles to enable them to embrace and really evangelise on the subject. It has become clear that without top-down engagement and belief then the customer experience will only ever be a small part of a balanced scorecard if it appears at all – at worst it will be a project given to someone in the organisation who has little or no chance of success, but at least they provide senior managers with a fig leaf to say that they are taking it seriously!

Remember to be successful any customer experience activity needs top-down support and bottom-up action and NEVER refer to it as a project or programme which shouts short term and someone else's issue

Education has also been a black hole with few training programmes making the leap from simple service training to the more encompassing customer experience agenda. Senior executive programmes rarely include the customer experience as part of the learning programme. The effect is felt both at the board level where executives are unsure 'how' they should engage with a customer experience agenda and lower down where the newly appointed Director of Customer Experience has no source to use as a guide for their role and often find themselves in a team of one as the organisational design does not have a convenient customer experience model.

Remember just appointing someone to a role with the word 'customer' in the title does not mean they are fully equipped to deliver in a customer experience role

Thankfully the business world is ready to embrace a new future where companies become more 'customer intelligent', which essentially means that they structure and manage their businesses in a way that optimises all of the information available to them about their customers and effectively balance the commercial needs with their customer expectations, creating a true 'win–win' position.

If you make the decision to focus on the customer in your strategy it's the start of a journey and the first question needs to be: 'can we identify who our customers really are?' So one of the start points is to ask: 'Who are your customers and what do they look like?'

This leads to endless hours of debate and discussion as different functions have their own names for customers – public relations have 'opinion formers', the group board have 'stakeholders', the sales team have 'clients' and 'prospects', and the retail team have 'customers'.

What needs to emerge is a picture of those customers that make up the bulk of your paying business, at the highest level – you have years to develop a whole segmentation so don't overthink this.

When you do develop segments of customers make sure that they are done with a strong human and visual element rather than statistics and trend analysis.

In an attempt to sort out this confusion one international business decided that customers were simply 'the people who actually pay the bills', and even that was then dissected and argued over.

The customer value proposition

Having established what your customer looks like you need to begin to understand their relative importance in your company and your customer engagement model? In traditional marketing terms you need to look at the customer value proposition (CVP) where your company is considering the three components of price, product and service – you can substitute customer experience for service. A CVP is 'the promise that value will be delivered and the belief from customers that value will be experienced'. It is not an advertising strapline or slogan and it must not make 'benefit assertions' that are not subsequently delivered or are so difficult for customers to access or experience that they are in effect meaningless.

Few, if any, businesses derive their CVP from an equal and high weighting along each of these three dimensions, as this is unrealistic. The CVP is determined by the relative focus on the three dimensions and while each of the three dimensions will be included one will always be dominant.

Remember a CVP should show the relative balance of importance of the key strategic drivers

Even those companies that have traditionally been seen as product businesses from high-tech lab equipment to major logistics companies are recognising that differentiation on the product level is no longer sustainable in the longer term and are dialling up the service/customer experience component of their emerging CVPs to a position of strategic dominance. Stepping up or evolving the customer component is the key.

Remember to turn the company on its head – which is the way too many companies have lurched – is not sustainable or deliverable

Having agreed on an enhanced role for the customer as part of the CVP your challenge is to find a means for delivering a differentiated

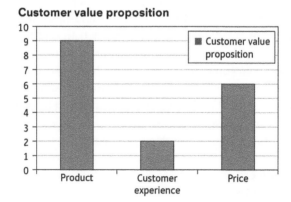

Customer value proposition

experience in areas that the customer values, track performance and identify areas for improvement to effectively drive business performance.

Remember customer experience activities and success should be directly connected to the bottom line of your business, otherwise why do it at all. Customer experience is not about an altruistic customer utopia, it is about combining customer experience with commercial sense

Building up knowledge about your customers

In order to do that we need to understand how a customer experiences the company and where the key points of interaction are that will influence and then drive the behaviour of that customer.

The backdrop for this is a customer journey map (CJM) that is an 'outside-in' customer view of how they experience the sector, product or service. When you ask companies if they have this view of the world many will say 'yes we do'. What emerges on closer inspection is that they have business process maps – these are *not* a CJM, they are an internal map of 'what *you do to* customers'. Making this leap of understanding can be difficult given the, often huge, scale of investment made in mapping internal processes. It is critical to understand the difference between an 'outside-in' and an 'inside-out' view.

Remember that process maps are NOT customer journey maps

Your company has the capability to take an 'outside-in' customer view and to create a customer journey map – it is there just waiting in the wings to be activated .The information needed to create your

CJM is locked up inside your company and we will unlock that when we explore how to create a CJM in Chapter 6.

The problem is that we tend to play a game of pass the parcel with customers – teams engage only during specific stages and then the customer moves on to another department to be managed – in this way we create disjointed, compartmentalised experiences which feel disjointed to the customer. Anyone who has experienced the cold handoff when we phone a call centre and have to repeat the same story to multiple people brings this into sharp relief.

Remember that every customer handoff during an interaction is an opportunity for dissatisfaction and negative emotions to develop

The development of CJM approaches over the last 10 years has now provided ready-made structures both in the process of creating and then refining the output of a CJM to allow your company to connect the parts of the company involved in the various stages into one end-to-end journey. The visual CJM provides you with a common view of the journey for the first time, a critical step to gaining alignment across the silos of your internal teams and to begin to understand interdependencies across teams in terms of the experience that customers have of your company.

Your CJM becomes the pivot around which experiences can be both visualised and designed. It allows you to centralise into a single point information that will be held in different parts of the businesss – connecting data, information, people and processes.

Remember the map itself is not the end deliverable, it is just a tool to build actions off and a reference point for future activity. Too many businesses produce a map and then

stop – if you are going to do that you are better off not even starting

Of course there remains a significant role for the underlying process mapping and engineering, but this should now be led by the customer journey map activity.

The impact of not being customer intelligent?

Let's consider an example of a business that is not displaying a customer intelligent approach. In a world where Disney continues to set the benchmark, this hotel has invested very significant sums in creating a potentially world-beating waterpark, both in terms of the physical rides and the advertising and marketing budget to promote it. Yet in terms of the end product, I would argue having experienced it that it is today a triumph of style over substance in experiential terms.

The expectations are set high by the slick and expensive advertising campaigns. Having purchased tickets I arrived with my family and having navigated the crowds found myself at the entry to the park. First problem was that I actually did not have actual tickets, I had tickets to get a ticket that meant a queue of around 20–30 minutes that no one had prepared me for, to arrive at one of the handful of counter points. The tension levels and frustration were rising. Having got to the front of the queue it appeared the only reason for this secondary ticketing was to provide an opportunity to sell me more. Having finally got into the park it was then unclear how it worked, people were wandering around with large inflatable rings – where did they come from, why do they have them, we wondered? Looking around there was no one to ask, not quite Disney where we would be falling over staff trying to predict that we needed something. Next the signage: once you got to the top of the rides there were different queues and different entrances – again creating unwanted confusion about which one was the right one. Finally there was little obvious shelter from the blazing sun or measures taken to ensure that visitors remained cool. The irony of the lack of staff was that when you looked into the water channel that flows around the park there were plenty of staff on hand – one can guess that drowning is a bit of a risk in this location and would result in some rather bad publicity, staff are deployed to ensure this does not happen.

A customer intelligent company would recognise these visitor issues and act on them as they are damaging the brand. The points to note here are that expectations were created both by the company advertising and the personal comparison to other high-end attractions that are not delivered in reality at this resort. The investment was in the infrastructure and not the experience and these shortcomings were very obvious and resolvable. In the short term just communicating with visitors to better manage their expectations around ticketing and scripting the ticket office conversation to provide better basic information about how the park functions would be a quick win.

Things to think about

If you want to be more customer intelligent you need to make better use of the assets that exist in the business today. The information needed to inform and create improved experiences exists but is too often fragmented and owned by different groups who do not talk to each other. You need to understand what information will be helpful to inform the experience and bring that together in a single location. This will include information about customer needs, value, expectations, measures and emotions.

My most commonly used analogy is to describe customer experiences as a theatre or film production. There are many parts behind the scenes from lighting to cinematography, to make up and scripts that all contribute to a successful outcome. These are unseen and not cared about by the audience who are there to enjoy the performance. Yet they would not expect the actors to be asked to work without a script, props, direction and a clear understanding of both the story and the outcome.

Customer experience has to be designed in the same way; it relies on many back office supporters but is ultimately about the delivery of an experience to the customer. While there is room for some ad lib, it should be seen as freedom within a framework where the emphasis is on the ability to consistently deliver at the key points of a customer journey.

3

Emotions or how you feel and the customer experience

The 'E' word is of course 'emotions' – a word with which we are all familiar, and to greater or lesser degrees comfortable either acknowledging or talking about. This is true in our private lives and this difficulty we feel in talking about emotions transfers into the business world. While it is undeniable that emotions play a part in our experiences they are too often seen as too difficult to address or just a by-product of an experience rather than the critical driver. It is much easier to design processes around rational behaviour – if we do this the rationally thinking customer will do this. The reality is that we need to think not only about the rational but also the irrational customer – one who enters an experience in a particular state of mind or whose state of mind changes during the interaction, and we need to recognise, plan for and respond to that. So we will consider:

- How do emotions impact your business results and bottom line?
- How can we connect emotions into experiences?
- How do emotions impact on your ability to achieve your aims in experiential terms?

The 'E' word is one often glossed over in corporate life as something too fluffy and unmeasurable to be considered. Yet it is emotion that drives significant activity. Put simply, while companies are generally uncomfortable trying to build in and understand the impact of emotions, so much of what happens is about how customers 'feel' and, hard as it is, emotions have to be considered seriously.

Processes seek to tell us that we should design for the rational customer – however, it is when we are at our most emotional and least rational that we make some of our biggest decisions. Understanding the emotional state of mind of a customer should change the way the company acts and behaves, and recognising this is a huge area of opportunity. This challenges some of the lean process thinking and is illustrated through real-life examples that all readers will be able to associate with.

Emotion in the automotive industry

We all know that car companies spend an incredible amount of money designing their vehicles. According to a Germany Trade & Invest report, Germany alone spent €17.6 billion in 2014 just on automotive research and development (R&D) – 93,000 (full-time equivalent) researchers are employed in the automotive R&D section in Germany alone. The issue is that the investment is in the design, manufacture and production of the physical vehicle – no doubt there is much love and attention and emotion built into those vehicles, but the same level of investment is not made in translating this into the experience of the end customer. You need to be confident that your experience is every bit as great as your product.

With this scale of investment and the incredible range of features and nuances built in to make the car stand out in a crowded market it is a challenge to convey these messages to the potential customer.

As an example, consider an engagement with a major car manufacturer in which you ask how many messages you would like to convey to a customer throughout the purchase life cycle.

As a team we brainstormed the list and it ran to over 100 different messages, from the price to the hook that holds the filler cap when you fill up, to the dashboard indicator light that shows which side of the car the fuel cap is (yes, most cars have that indicator light today and even some of the manufacturer's own team didn't know it!).

We then listed the opportunities to communicate them; through the website/media when the potential customer researches independently; when they arrive on the forecourt; when they have a test drive; when they buy the car and then when they collect and drive away. That gives around five opportunities to transmit the messages:

1. Visit the website

2. Read media/brochure

3. First forecourt visit

4. Test drive

5. Collect car.

Some messages are more important than others so we then ranked them and began to work out where it was best to give the messages.

We then checked this against what actually happens today. One thing the team had in the current experience was a checklist at the point of vehicle handover that was used by the forecourt team to ensure they had passed on what was deemed to be critical information. This was literally ticked off and then the customer was asked to sign to say they understood – completion of these tick lists was also a key metric and created a notional 'green light' on the individual scorecard.

This approach is not unique and will be being mirrored around the world as we speak. The process of a checklist makes perfect sense if you discard the emotional state of the customer, a fact reinforced by my own experience with another car brand weeks later when I acquired a new car. In this case the checklist at opportunity 5 above (collect car) had around 30 items on it from how the in-car computer works, through to how to change the clock and use the electric tow bar – and finally, yes, the lamp that tells me which side the filler cap is and how to open it! As he attempted to force feed me this information, as part of the process, all I wanted to do was escape the forecourt and drive my new car. As the minutes dragged by, my frustration levels grew. I was excited about my new car and not in receive mode at that moment – in the end he was hanging through the driver's door window trying to explain more and more until I said, 'Where do I need to sign?' He rather sadly indicated a line at the bottom of the page that I immediately signed without reading and cheerily waved him goodbye. The simple fact is that I was not in the right 'state of mind' to listen to what he wanted me to, even though it was helpful. No doubt someone else has experienced the same thing and then rather embarrassingly gone to fill up the car and not been able to open the filler cap! The challenge at that point is to impart the minimum information for me to be safe and not embarrassed at the filling station, so basic controls like lights, windscreen wipers/washers, brakes and of course the filler cap release!

In experiential terms that also means that a really important interaction was not maximised in terms of creating a positive memory of the dealership experience. What should have been a celebration of the purchase turned into an exercise in escape.

If you look at experiences through the emotional lens and consider the mental state of your customer as part of that, then you design a very different experience. If you actively design the end-to-end experience of that segment of the journey you will end up with a differentiated experience that works for the customer and the employee.

In this case, particularly with higher-end sales, the innovation in terms of the experience solution was to offer a follow-up visit by one of the experts to answer any questions that you might have – two weeks in you have tried the basics – both to reinforce knowledge and to add in a couple of things that you wouldn't otherwise have known. The silver lining being that there is another legitimate opportunity to engage with the customer post sale and reinforce that positive brand memory.

Remember the old ones are the best when it comes to quotes and here is a classic from the late great Maya Angelou, who said: 'I've learned that people will forget what you said, people will forget what you did, but people will never forget how you made them feel'

Recognising the value of emotions

The Maya Angelou quote goes with me everywhere and it plays absolutely to the heart of the customer experience. It is a principle that can be used to drive decision making *in terms of customer experience – we are in the memories business.*

In customer experience terms we need to take account of emotions at two levels, one of which is reactive and the other proactive.

On the one hand we need to be aware and predict how customers are likely to be feeling at particular interaction points. This will be outside the control of the company but will be key to how the experience is delivered. If the customer is likely to be nervous, the experience should be set out to reassure; if the customer is going to be excited, we need to build on that excitement; if the customer is going to be agitated, we need to be calm, collected and confident.

On the other hand we plan to create an emotional reaction from the customer – which could be positive surprise: 'that was much easier than I thought it was going to be'; or it could be joy or fun; or perhaps it could be relief. The point is that we can do this by recognising the likely emotional state of the customer as they begin the interaction and we can plan for a positive outcome.

In both cases we need to understand and react to or create emotional reactions from customers. In order to do this we have to actively design that experience with an emotional outcome in mind and then equip people to deliver on that outcome through training, skills, access to data and systems, and then measure the results.

It is through this approach that customer experience professionals can show their company that experiences that are designed are not necessarily more expensive, and in most cases can be executed at little or no cost and be connected to the bottom line.

Emotion in financial services

When considering the practicality and value of how to input emotional understanding into actively designing an experience, consider the following example.

An insurance company was selling general insurance to small retail businesses and wanted to sell in a rider to the core policy in the form of 'continuity insurance'– award yourself a gold star if you have any idea what this actually is! (If not, the answer is: 'it covers the loss of income that a business suffers after a disaster. The income loss covered may be due to disaster-related closing of the business facility or due to the rebuilding process after a disaster.')

The sales of the rider were not as good as the company expected and they couldn't quite understand why such a valuable additional cover was so often rejected by customers? The calls were largely scripted so by listening to call recordings and reading the script it was possible to identify where the call was failing both the customer and the company.

Most customers contacting an insurance company are in defensive mindset – the industry seems to almost pride itself on impenetrable language and confusion. Who would ever call the price of the service a 'premium', suggesting it is higher priced than normal? In this situation the customer wants to feel they have some form of control and does not want to appear stupid or naive.

With this emotional context it was clear that when an agent, after selling the basic package, asked 'would you like to buy continuity insurance?' the customers rejected the opportunity not because it was a bad idea, but because rather than appear stupid by asking what it was they simply defaulted to 'no thanks'. Listening to the calls both the slight momentary hesitation and the way people said 'errr, no thanks' told you they didn't actually know what they were turning down but were too embarrassed to ask. The agents faced a further problem because they were working on the standard call centre measure of call duration, meaning that they just took the first answer and moved on in order not to exceed the allotted call time.

Working with the agents, removing the internal barriers around key performance indicators (KPIs) and putting the customer emotion of potential embarrassment into the mix, the call was redesigned. The agents were asked to describe what was meant by 'continuity insurance' using a story to illustrate how it helped a customer. Using these anecdotes, instead of 'would you like to buy continuity insurance?', the call was redesigned to take away the customer embarrassment. Now it went more along the lines of: 'Would you like to buy continuity insurance? Before you decide can I just take a moment to explain what continuity insurance actually means as I found it a little confusing when I started . . . [insert your favourite customer example].' The call duration was extended which was a negative in terms of lean process, but the potential for conversion was significantly improved.

Cost to the business was low: implementation was easy and quick, staff felt more engaged and listened to, the customers were more informed, and the overall experience improved.

Financial services provides a perfect environment for customer experience to thrive as a positive driver of brand loyalty. However, in countless surveys they appear at the lower end of the customer experience league tables, with the exception of the US insurer USAA, which has consistently bucked the trend and shown that you can create really positive experiences in the sector.

Of all companies, in customer experience terms you could say that ironically insurance companies are truly blessed. An industry that is run by accountants and actuaries and talks non-stop about numbers and risk profiles actually has an amazing emotional proposition to deliver.

Insurance companies have what many businesses would love to have – their customers calling them at a real time of need, of heightened emotions driven by pain, worry, vulnerability. When you have an accident or a problem with damage to your property or have lost a valuable item, often you will call the insurer before even your family. You are in a heightened emotional state and what happens over those first few minutes and then beyond will truly shape your decision making about loyalty (or not) to the company, and beyond that your advocacy to friends and family.

The rational versus irrational

It was noted in the introduction to this chapter that rational and irrational are key components in the emotional debate. Traditionally, companies plan and 'design' processes that are linear, they make assumptions about how the rational person will respond and seek to minimise the number of steps to drive efficiency.

Most business process mapping uses the company need as the key arbiter, and does not take into account how a customer might be 'feeling' at any one moment and how those feelings might need to be addressed.

For example, in process map terms having 10 days of 'white space' between making an application for credit or a mortgage is not a problem (I define 'white space' as a period when there is no communication with the customer – this could be measured in minutes, hours, days or weeks depending on the interaction; it could also be characterised as that awkward silence that we all recognise from day-to-day life). In process map terms it is represented by a straight line on a page between request and response, but in emotion terms the customer is desperate for contact. Even a holding note could have an exponential impact in terms of reducing stress and improving how the customer feels at this point of high stress and tension. Recognising this emotional vulnerability, one financial services company sent text messages informing the customer that their mortgage application had moved from Department X to Department Y, reassuring the customer that the application was progressing.

The other assumption that companies make when creating their customer-facing processes is that when we enter their company space, whether physically or virtually, we adopt a persona which means we are going to 'act as a customer in their world would'. Suddenly I am thinking like a rational and perhaps knowledgeable mobile phone customer or logistics customer, but of course I don't take on that persona: I am still Alan and still have all the other issues that I face, and other things on my mind which the company is never aware of.

Personas

One solution to this is to create personas which represent the customer, these are typically pen picture portraits of the customer group which describe in some detail the characteristics of that particular customer group. They can include pictures of the typical customer, details on their domestic and business life, age – however, once again they rarely include emotional content, how that particular person feels themselves in specific situations and relative to other customer groups. Personas should have a strong emotional overlay if they are going to truly reflect the customer. For example, how do they 'feel' about technology; are they time rich or time poor; and how does that impact on how they 'feel' about elements of the customer experience? And for an insurance example, considering how upset and even distraught a customer might be at the point of contact.

Remember a customer is not a 'blank sheet of paper' when they engage with your experience

Choosing where to focus on emotions

It is not possible, practical or necessary to design all experiences for all emotional eventualities. Viewing house details in a property search is not going to be a priority interaction when it comes to introducing emotions; the day of moving into a new home would be the right time.

By definition, a moment of truth or a pain point in the customer experience is characterised by a heightened emotional state and it is possible to predict the likely state of mind of the majority of customers at those trigger points and introduce that as a key driver of design and process at those points. When starting on this emotional journey, as we identified earlier it is relatively straightforward to isolate which interactions merit real focus on the emotional component – both what the customer is feeling and what you want them to feel during and post the interaction.

Customer experience disaster recovery

While the idea of getting inside the irrational mind of a customer may seem difficult, the reality is that it is not and once there we can rapidly create scenarios that will become trainable executions in the workplace. Recognising that failures will happen and preparing for the situation is not an organisational weakness, rather it should be seen as an organisational strength. In the same way that companies have 'disaster recovery plans' for everything from a computer meltdown to the offices being destroyed by fire, companies should have disaster recovery plans for bad experiences.

Not every experience needs a recovery plan but where there is a high risk to business of that failure then it is required. If a major IT system fails what will the front of house team do?

Back in my retail days when electronic till systems were relatively new we had a disaster recovery experience in case of power outage. An experience I was called on to use more than once! It was simple: we closed the doors, asked people to stop shopping and make their way to the tills – at that point the team at the checkouts would estimate the value of the shopping, always erring on the low side, and then agree that with the customer. Thankfully in those days it was always cash or cheque so payment was easy. The customers, while sometimes unhappy at not being able to complete their 'shopping task', were nevertheless delighted to have got what they always saw as a bargain. We turned what could have been a bad experience into something better and more memorable.

In companies today major project investments that will go through an investment appraisal should have a section covering the 'customer experience what ifs', which can cover both initial deployment and then ongoing operational.

All chief financial officers should be aware of the business risk of an adverse impact on customers when customers make decisions based on emotional reactions to a problem rather than necessarily logic. Just think about the issues facing the car manufacturer VW following the disclosures about cheating emission tests and the customer emotional reaction to this loss of trust.

When O2, the UK arm of the Telefónica mobile telephone company, had an outage on their mobile network that impacted huge numbers of customers, and garnered column inches in the media, they had a disaster to deal with. While the first issue was the technical fix, the second was the impact on customer trust in the reliability of their service and the potential for mass defection. In response and by way of apology, regardless of whether you were directly impacted the company issued all O2 customers with a credit for use against O2 products.

There will be executives that would see that kind of response as 'avoidable cost' or 'high risk' and would therefore never deliver on that unwritten aspect of a company promise. That emotional bond between customer and company that far exceeds any mission statement or values list or even regulatory 'requirement to provide compensation'. While I am unaware of the redemption rate, from experience, it will have been low in reality but the gesture carried significant weight with customers. A company showing an emotion-based reaction and humility will linger in the memory.

Remember having customer experience defined as a key risk on the company risk register is a great way to raise the profile and secure budget approval for customer experience developments

Things to think about

Emotions are a critical part of customer experience design thinking. Companies that fail to both recognise and act on the emotional component of their experience are creating a significant business risk which can be formally captured in the risk register.

It could be claimed that Facebook tapped into the basic human emotion when they introduced the very simple 'like' button into their customer world.

Emotions drive behaviours and actions that directly connect to the bottom line of the company on both sides of the balance sheet. On the revenue side, when we are emotionally connected or where positive memories are created, the propensity to buy more and stay longer is going to be increased. On the cost side, there are a number of impacts from the reduction in staff churn to the reduction in customer complaints and therefore cost to serve.

Emotions are exponentially relevant at critical moments in the customer life cycle. These should be identified and specific attention given to understanding the emotional components of those interactions, and active design of the experience is then required.

Part

2

Customer experience in action

4

Where are you? What do you want to deliver?

This chapter looks at how companies can undertake a quick assessment of the current state of their customer experience, set targets for where they want to get to and ensure that there is the required alignment within the business both vertically and horizontally.

The first step in any customer-based work is to ensure that your company is very clear, top to bottom, on the actual experience that you want to deliver to your customers; you can then assess how well you are actually delivering that. By looking carefully, but quickly, at the customer interactions and at the resources in place today you can ensure that activities and resources align in delivering that experience.

So you need to understand your current level of maturity, what assets you have in place and where you want the customer interventions to take the business.

Many companies also lack some basic information on the actual experience that they want to deliver. For instance, you need to understand how or if your mission, vision and values connect to your customer experience and then you need to be able to align targets for where you want to get to and ensure that there is alignment within the business, both vertically and horizontally.

Having recognised that you want to move forward on delivering an enhanced customer experience as a vital component of your overall business strategy you will need to answer some critical questions.

- What is our current state of maturity in terms of our customer experience capability?

- Where do we believe we need to get to in terms of our customer experience capability in order to deliver on our business plan?
- Are we clear on what customer experience we want to deliver?

These may seem like simple questions, but if you think about your company today could you answer them with any degree of confidence? What you will also find is that even if you have a view on the answers it is almost certain that colleagues in different parts of the organisation will have different views. Different views are in part driven by your location, your daily activity, your position and department in the company and partly based on your personal expectations both in terms of what the company should be doing and what you have visibility of. Those that are closest to the end customer inevitably have a clearer view on the current experience. It is important to look for some alignment of these often quite differing views at the outset. In effect we must level set the views across the business and ensure that we all have a common start point. This is also an opportunity to do some foundational work, which will be very useful as the journey moves into planning, mapping and design work.

Remember a customer experience is not an input: it is the output of activities inside your company

Let's consider how to answer the three questions in more detail.

What is our current state of maturity in terms of our customer experience capability and where do we need to get to?

There are two sources of information on where you are today, what your customers tell you and what your company tells you. Each will have a view on how mature the experience is, but from different perspectives typically your staff will tell you how it feels to deliver the experience and your customers will tell you how it feels to be a customer. You will also most likely uncover some conflicts of interest, for example between policies and procedures in place to ensure a 'clean internal audit' and what you actually say you want to do in terms of the customer experience.

Your company probably has a lot of information on the customer view through the reams of ongoing market research programmes, but is less likely to understand your colleague views. For this reason, and because it is key to engage the company at an early stage, I always recommend you begin with an internal view of maturity.

The first step is to agree through a simple online survey for colleagues where in the timeline of customer experience maturity your company sits today. I have found it useful to have a simple overall segmentation at this stage, with supporting information. It can be displayed as a four-segment circle that offers the options of starting, evolving, maturing or maintaining.

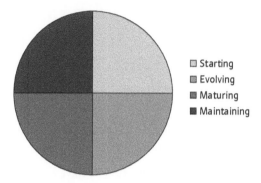

- □ Starting
- ▨ Evolving
- ▩ Maturing
- ■ Maintaining

If the overall questions were about defining the stage in the timeline that you occupy, what other supporting evidence would it be good to understand and how would you check if there is alignment across the company in different departments and different levels?

You will often find that there are different views based on where you sit in the customer journey; for example, the acquiring and on-boarding of a customer may be well invested in as a business priority, but once a customer progresses over time the standards of experience may be significantly degraded. So the ability to segment the responses based on where in the customer journey the respondent operates can be very helpful.

To determine the answer to the single question of where we are in terms of our overall customer experience journey you need to gather data across a range of key areas. It is very tempting at this point to load a wide range of questions into a survey but you should avoid this, it will dilute the volume and quality of the responses and you will have many more opportunities to gather more granular information as you need it in order to define or support decisions about the customer experience.

My approach is to look at the key drivers of your customer experience and then to isolate a handful of questions that will act as a good guide to the current position. Ideally we are looking for no more than 10 questions at this stage; you can go deeper later.

Remember you can ask further questions at any point so do not overload surveys with questions that fall into the 'nice to know' but not going to be actionable in the near future category

The key areas for you to focus on at this stage are all high level and can be broken down into the following:

- Customer strategy – do you have one?
- Brand strategy – what expectation are you setting?
- Customer knowledge – what do you know about key needs?
- Business processes – how is the customer view included?
- Customer data – what and how is it used?
- IT infrastructure – do you have a consolidated view of the customer experience?
- Measures – what customer metrics exist and what do they achieve?
- People – who is engaged and how is that achieved?

The problem is that if you send a survey out asking about words like 'strategy' and 'infrastructure' it creates lots of confusion at different levels of the business, so the language used needs to work for different levels and departments.

Over the years I have seen various combinations of questions and language to overcome this very real barrier to getting meaningful feedback. My suggestions based on that are as follows:

1. The company clearly explains to all staff the importance of the customer experience that it wants to deliver.

2. The company sets clear expectations about the experience its customers should expect.

3. The company understands the touch-points that are the most important for customers.

4. The company gives enough emphasis to the injection of the desired customer experience into the key business processes.

5. The company uses enough customer data to guide the design of the most important touch-points.

6. The company makes customer information available through a single view.

7. The company has clear links between customer measures and customer outcomes.

8. The company uses customer feedback to identify and deliver experience improvements.

9. The company has behaviours, competencies and training identified to enable staff to deliver the desired customer experience.

10. The company spends enough time communicating direction and taking a visible lead from senior executives in terms of customer experience.

We are asking the respondents to describe the extent to which they agree or disagree with each of the 10 statements.

Offer a scale of 1–5:

1. Strongly agree

2. Somewhat agree

3. Neither agree nor disagree

4. Somewhat disagree

5. Strongly disagree.

In each case, the questions should be followed by an optional free text box using the statement and a catch-all free text at the end for other comments:

Optional: Please describe why you chose this answer.

The free text is helpful in giving context to the scores and to see if consistent themes emerge that are impacting on the scores either positively or negatively.

A simple way to gather this information is to use an online survey tool – there are plenty to choose from and you only need basic functionality:

- ability to load questions and set a scale for the responder to use;
- ability to load basic information about the responder, e.g. gender, age, length of service, department, job grade, etc.;
- ability to have qualitative free text box responses;
- ability to perform simple segmentation of the data within the tool and output simple reports.

You could consider tools such as SurveyMonkey, KeySurvey, SurveyGizmo and others, all of which are easy to use and low cost.

When conducting these surveys it is key to be able to preserve anonymity to give you the best chance of getting honest answers. While you may not use all of the individual data, it is worth collecting at this stage in order to cover the future eventuality of someone senior asking a question that you need to be able to respond to! For example, is there a difference in view between those who are new to the company and those who have longer service?

One really great way to engage your wider internal team and condition them to receiving regular surveys on the customer experience is to ask people, as part of the first survey, to volunteer to be on a staff panel. You set the expectations at the outset: why join, what will it mean and what will I get out of it?

Remember if you set up an internal research panel this is a commitment and you need to use it regularly and feed back to the team

This an example of a draft email that you could use:

Dear Colleague,

I am really excited to announce the launch of the Company X Peoples Panel. We really value your knowledge and expertise and need your help to shape future decisions on behalf of our customers. It is really easy: all you need to do is click the link below and join our Company X Panel – we will be issuing short questionnaires once a month for you to complete. This will take no more than 10 minutes of your time each month and will be invaluable in shaping our future customer experiences. We will provide regular feedback on the findings and how they are contributing to our customer experience improvements.

This has the potential to begin to create an internal community and unleash some of that pent up capability – colleagues will self-identify an interest and you can, over time, add in other forums for them to discuss the customer experience on a more regular basis. You will get feedback in real time from a cross section of departments that will help to raise the profile of the customer experience across the company.

Next, select your audience: this could be an all person company survey or you may want to select individuals. If you choose the latter option you need to ensure that you include all senior managers (to avoid upsetting people!) plus a representative sample covering all departments and levels relative to their size. One way to do this is to determine that you want a survey of 30 per cent of the company and ask personnel to identify 30 per cent of the people from each department and across grades. As you can see, the better option is to make this an all company experience!

Having issued the survey, the next step is to collate the data from the responses and feed that back to both the senior team and respondents initially and then the wider company.

Remember the aim of the survey is to understand the current perceived state maturity and to use it to move towards a common view of both the

current and the required future levels of maturity/competence

Evaluating the scores

At a simple level take the scores from across the question set and at a question level grade the answers. Where the average score is 1 or 2 you can place the company in the 'starting' stage; where it is 3 'evolving'; 4 is 'maturing'; and 5 is 'maintaining'. Then take the scores for all of the questions and create an overall score for the company.

The best way to feed the information back to the senior team is through a 2–3-hour workshop session – this can be the board or the board and direct reports. You present the information in two parts.

1. First take the senior team view showing the average score across each of the 10 questions. Provide a short digest of the qualitative comments to give context for the scoring.

   - Take each question in turn and ask the team to review that score and agree if it is right or wrong in terms of the current position. Discuss until they reach consensus – you will have different views in the room.

2. Then ask the question 'what would it take for us to achieve our two-year business goals?' Revisit each question and discuss where on the scale the results would need to be.

   - Review the answers and decide as a team where on the scale the company is today: is it starting, evolving, maturing or maintaining in terms of the overall company customer journey maturity.

Having agreed this then it is both revealing and fun to look at what the rest of the company said so create a side by side set of scores for each of the 10 questions showing the wider business scores. Highlight some of the qualitative feedback to give context around why the staff disagrees with the senior leadership view! You will find some, often significant, differences in views from the top to those across the company. Be prepared to break down the results into different groups or segments to illustrate where the key variances are.

Discuss the reasons why these variances might have occurred. If they are based on the wider company view ask the team whether they want to amend their final scoring – experience tells me that they rarely do!

In my experience most companies will find themselves in the 'starting' and at best 'evolving' stage. If not, then I suggest you look hard and challenge the evidence for a more advanced level of maturity. This is where the wider company input can be used to offset the usually ambitious and exaggerated view of the senior team.

The purpose of this discussion is to raise awareness that communication on customer experience may be an issue in the company.

Remember it is often the case that activity is in place or happening, but there is no visibility beyond the immediate delivery team

Now you have a leadership consensus on the current and future state at this high level. This provides a platform to begin to dig into the detail of the current customer experience.

You need to communicate the results of the discussions back to those who gave up their time to take part in the original survey and outline what the next steps will be.

This is all part of raising the profile of the customer inside the business. Get the CEO or a senior executive to sign off on the communication to connect the leadership to the customer messages

Remember communicate, communicate, communicate and use the word customer as much as possible

The next piece of the 'where are we today?' puzzle is to understand what activity is currently under way that is either badged or designed to directly impact on the customer experience. You need to know what the activity is called, what its objectives are, how and which customer it is designed to impact, when it is due to deliver and if possible the budget.

Create a simple spreadsheet to capture this information. This will be invaluable as we progress and identify opportunities to improve – as a simple step, check are they already in scope of an initiative, will it deliver in time, is there already budget available and other useful insights.

If you have a programme support office, this is often a good starting point to gather the information. If not, monthly reporting packs can be a source, or you need to talk to teams across the business to determine what is under way or in the planning phase.

Are we clear on what customer experience we want to deliver?

Most companies will have a mission statement, a vision and values along with statements about the brand and what it stands for. Very few of my clients over the years have been able to answer the following question: 'Could you please describe the key characteristics of the customer experience that you want your teams to deliver?'

Ask yourself the question, write down the answer and see how that compares if you ask colleagues within your business. If the leaders cannot answer the question consistently what hope is there for the rest of the company?

As an example, what does this often-used answer actually mean: 'We want our people to be passionate about the customer'? How does it translate into something relevant and meaningful within finance or customer service or the boardroom? How can anyone in the company be held to account if there is no clear customer experience delivery framework or touchstones that they can use to test their actions?

The actual customer experience that you want to deliver is derived from the business strategy, brand and company values, the mission statement and the vision statement. You need access to all of these documents as inputs to creating your customer experience design guide (CEDG).

Defining your customer experience

You should describe what the company would provide to its customers in terms of a customer experience. This is a qualitative statement – it should draw from the brand and corporate positioning and not be detached from them.

Remember that your mission, vision and values can be meaningless without a clear description of your required customer experience that, in essence, ensures alignment with the most important element, i.e. the people upon whom everyone depends: management to get paid, investors to get returns, bankers to get repaid, governments to get taxes, etc.

Remember, unless there is a clear linkage between the customer experience description and the rest there is a risk of disconnect

So firstly you need to collate the company mission, vision, values and brand positioning and the overall strategic plan statement.

You also need to be very clear on the purpose of your company to avoid being reduced to the level of tasks. For example, at Disney the purpose for all is 'creating the magic' – everything else is a task, from sweeping the road to parking cars, that together are designed to achieve that purpose. Too often we focus on tasks and not the purpose and then short-term tasks take control.

- What is your company purpose?
- The component parts of your mission, vision and values all contribute to the business purpose.

- The overall purpose is usually captured in the mission and vision and describes why the company exists.
- The corporate strategy describes the business ambition – where it wants to get to.
- The key strategic drivers describe what the business needs to focus on.
- The brand strategy describes the behaviours that will be cascaded from the senior leadership.
- The values will describe the employee values that will be role modelled from the top.

Your description of the customer experience you want to deliver and the customer design guide will underpin these and allow the company to define in words what experience it needs to deliver in order to deliver on each of those components and will provide the capability to deliberately design the supporting customer journeys.

Your description of your desired customer experience will become the 'North Star' of the customer experience: it describes the experience that you want to deliver and out of that you will then derive your CDEG which you will use to design your experiences. It will connect your strategic platform to the reality of what your customers will experience.

The customer experience team should complete this work with input from as many different teams as possible. The leadership, as this is a key plank of your customer experience strategy, must endorse this, as this will be used to define future experiences.

You need to be very positive in tone and refer directly to the experience that the company delivers. The best way to do this is to use the following words as the start point and then complete the sentence in a way that truly reflects the other elements as described above.

'We *insist* that our customers will have an experience that . . . '

Try not to use more than 10–20 words (excluding my introduction line) – the purpose is to think hard about every word you use and ensure that your statement has meaning.

Here are a couple of sample descriptions:

> 'We *insist* that our customers will have an experience that is based on *trust* and is so *simple* that they can *enjoy* the life they choose.'

> 'We *insist* that our customers will have an experience that makes an *emotional* and *memorable connection* by being *passionate, inspiring, personal* and *unique.*'

Having established and agreed your desired customer experience you need to consider some key words that will bring the description to life and that can be crafted into your customer experience design guide. I first saw a version of this thinking in a UK financial services business some years ago.

Define no more than three to five words that will bring the description to life at a more granular level.

For example, if we take the first description above then we might choose to use the following as the next level of detail:

- **easy** – consistent, hassle-free choices to suit the customer;
- **personal** – offering flexible, relevant service recognising our customer;
- **trusted** – honest, deliver what we promise.

In each case ask yourself: are these deliverable? Setting goals that are overambitious at this stage is setting yourself and the company up to fail.

Remember you can change the words and evolve them as the business matures

Customer experience design guide

The final part of this stage of plan preparation is to define the actual customer experience design guide. This is an articulation of how the customer experience will be brought to life and set out the challenges or 'touchstones' that you and colleagues can refer to when you are making decisions – you can use them to test if you are really staying true to your purpose.

For them to be useful at a day-to-day level they need to be easy to remember and easily applied so we are looking for no more than three to five very short, one-line challenges.

If we take the example above of the desired customer experience and the supporting words we can then see how the challenges can be connected in.

'We *insist* that our customers will have an experience that is based on *trust* and is so *simple* that they can *enjoy* the life they choose.'

- **easy** – consistent, hassle-free choices to suit the customer;
- **personal** – offering flexible, relevant service recognising our customer;
- **trusted** – honest, deliver what we promise.

Easy – a common way to describe the word easy in a design guide is 'make the complex simple'. This is often used in financial service companies where the complexity ranges from product information to the language used (e.g. derivatives, continuity insurance) to the actual paperwork.

Personal – this can be described as ensuring that you have a 'human touch' involved in the experience. As an example, an online-only retailer sent my gift item and included a handwritten note from the person who dealt with the order. This was a brilliant way to make an anonymous purchase personal.

Trusted – this can be considered as a way of ensuring that the customer promise set by the brand is always delivered so 'always meet or exceed customer expectations'.

Remember when you are thinking about customer experience design guides you are wearing the customer hat and thinking, for example, *truly* how simple have we made this?

So we now have the agreed customer experience articulated and the customer experience design guide that together are the North Star and the day-to-day touchstones to use in the subsequent stages of the plan.

Desired customer experience

'We *insist* that our customers will have an experience that is based on *trust* and is so *simple* that they can *enjoy* the life they choose.'

- **easy** – consistent, hassle-free choices to suit the customer;
- **personal** – offering flexible, relevant service recognising our customer;
- **trusted** – honest, deliver what we promise.

Customer experience design guide

- Make the complex simple.
- Deliver a human touch.
- Always meet or exceed our customer expectations.

We will see how these are applied in Chapter 7 on designing customer experiences.

Things to think about

By completing these steps you now have the business discussing the customer using some basic but common language – you have achieved the first stage of alignment of views both in terms of where you are today and where you need to get to in order to meet future business targets. This second point is important because you are already tying the customer agenda into the business goals of the company.

You have also created some new business assets that are critical to the next stages of the development of the customer component of the business plan, including a customer project audit.

▶

You now have, often for the first time, your clear description of what experience the company wants to deliver to its customers. You also have the supporting design guide that will enable that statement, or North Star, to be activated inside the business through the active design and redesign of critical interactions.

We are now ready for the next stage: that is, to develop the plan for deploying customer-based change into the company.

5

How to plan the delivery of an improved customer experience

What is the sequence of events that needs to take place to begin to drive customer change? How is this sustained over an extended period to effect real change to the culture of the company? This chapter focuses in on 100 tiny changes as my mantra for customer change – it will talk about how large-scale customer activities struggle to get traction in established organisations, and explore some simple ideas to ensure that change is monitored, measured and celebrated. It will discuss the role of the leadership and middle management in the delivery of sustained change in the wider context of the company, and discuss creating confidence to act.

When you set off to build your customer experience journey plan there are three simple questions that you can ask yourself:

- Where are we today?
- Where do we want to get to?
- Do we have a map that shows where we want to get to as a business?

As you now move into this more structured approach through the creation of a plan, you will no doubt need to adapt the tools and formats to your own company, so please feel free to do so.

Remember in Chapter 1 where we discussed how a focus on the customer experience is often a reaction to negative news? Well you must keep that in mind when you get started.

This is not the best state of mind to be embarking on a customer experience change plan as it is already positioned as a distress option. We 'need' to focus on our customer rather than we 'want' to focus on our customer. Psychologically this creates negative energy that can roll over into the poor execution of the strategy and a ready willingness to abandon the approach as soon as better trading times return. One way around this is to push the message that through listening to customers it is clear that they will respond positively to you focusing more on what they want and need.

Remember to be successful it is absolutely key to ensure that the early plan is based on delivering quick wins to create a positive response and build confidence – if the plan is based on deliverables one to three years out it will never come to fruition

Your mantra for change in the customer experience world is 100s and then 1000s of tiny changes

In any plan you will always have small changes and bigger more challenging components. Too often the focus is on the big change activity that will deliver through a huge, heavily governed programme with a delivery window perhaps two or more years out. We need to invert this approach to drive a successful customer experience improvement plan. We are looking for lots of small changes which may be as simple as changing the wording of a standard letter to adjusting an existing measure. We are looking for a plan that embraces as wide an audience as possible and is relevant to as many people as possible. It will be the sheer volume and weight of these tiny changes that will, over time, improve both the customer and colleague experience and shift the culture. Why adopt this approach? The reality of any large company is that you are always running just to stand still and the pressure for resources is always high. The focus of effort tends to be on a few large programmes that are designed to deliver significant change. Customer experience improvement does not fit this format: it is more dynamic and as such requires a different approach to deployment; it is about wide reach and cultural impact rather than a single-point fixed deliverable like a new system deployment; it is about shifting your mindset to think about who is actually in control, who it is that can make changes in the business, and how much control the customer needs to have.

As I said at the start of this chapter, when you set off to build your customer experience journey plan there are three simple questions that you can ask yourself:

- Where are we today?
- Where do we want to get to?
- Do we have a map that shows where we want to get to as a business?

These same three questions apply to your customer journey and you are going to be looking at this from two perspectives: outside in, which is the customer view of the experience; and inside out, which is the internal view of the experience. The outside in will lead and the inside out will follow with changes to the way the company operates.

As we saw in Chapter 4, 'where are we today?' needs to be considered from both perspectives. By understanding these two sides of the same coin you will be well positioned to move to the next stage of identifying where you want or need to get to. Without this wider understanding you will find yourself engaged in a bunch of tactical experience 'fixes' which may be individually valuable but will not gross up to substantive and sustainable change.

It will be no surprise to learn that where there is a strong and structured internal view on the customer experience the outside-in view tends to be better too!

Understanding the context

Beginning with the inside-out view on where we are you need to gather some basic evidence that will provide the start point for the forward plan. In Chapter 4 we described how to gather basic information on current state experience maturity and to gain alignment on that high-level assessment of both current and future state customer experience and a view on the current customer projects in flight. In addition you can now look at key documents that will further reflect the level of customer activity and give further context to the current state plan. Here is a guide on typical documents that you can use – they may be called something different in your company:

- the strategic plan, one to three years
- brand documentation, e.g. values, promises
- the marketing plan
- the market research plan
- the monthly financial reporting
- the company KPIs by department
- the internal investment appraisal terms of reference
- organisation charts.

These documents – combined with your customer experience description, your customer experience maturity outputs and your customer experience design guide – provide an ideal input to the plan.

Rarely will you need new inputs: the idea is to draw the customer experience plan from the already-existing internal materials. In effect you are consolidating what already exists but is currently fragmented by department, function or team. This is important because you are not seen to be adding to the business workload.

How to review the key documents

In each case you are looking for evidence that the customer experience has specific focus so that you can be seen to be objective in your findings. To do this you can simply highlight in the documents where there is evidence that the customer experience is being taken into account as a specific deliverable, consideration or outcome in terms of measures. You are also looking at some early and obvious opportunities to highlight improvements.

Remember start to build a list of the opportunities and issues that you uncover during this stage of the planning

This stage is about understanding the big picture, gaining knowledge and starting to connect the different teams' engagement levels with the customer experience. Try asking these simple questions:

- Does the organisation have a team dedicated to the customer experience or is responsibility spread across a range of teams and departments? Who are the key players?
- Do the monthly company metrics connect to the customer? What, if any, actions are taken and tracked to show improvements month on month?
- Do leaders know the top five complaints and do they change?

The investment appraisal criterion is a key document to review. You are looking for evidence that when significant investments (capital or revenue) that merit review under the investment appraisal criteria are presented, there is a requirement to demonstrate the impact on end customers both during any change programme and after deployment. How many major IT infrastructure investments have caused massive disruption and damage to the customer experience even if only short term? Is the potential cost of this disruption highlighted in the business case, and are mitigating plans required?

This can be a simple and effective early win for the customer experience team. Through simple additions to an existing process you can have a significant impact on how the business thinks about investment in the future. This is not about stopping investments and development but injecting a customer viewpoint at the commercial level and beginning to influence the culture as a consequence.

You simply add a couple of key questions, for example:

- Can you demonstrate how you have assessed any potential impacts on the customer experience during this deployment?
- What will the impact of this investment be on the ongoing customer experience?

- What plans exist to manage short-term negative impacts on the customer experience?
- How will the impact on the customer experience be measured and monitored?
- Investigate and describe the upstream and downstream impact of what we plan to do on later interactions – how will what we do be impacted by earlier interactions?

As a further example, how connected is the marketing plan and campaign activity to the customer service team that will be delivering the experience? Too often do we see a marketing campaign launch that creates a huge spike in demand that the call centre is not geared up to handle. This creates a poor service level, poor experience and internal frustration and even anger! This is another quick win simply through ensuring that internal connectivity is happening,

This knowledge is particularly helpful as you engage with the business and you are able to demonstrate a solid understanding of current customer-based activity whether planned or in flight already. Nothing undermines your position and confidence in the customer experience team more than someone being able to say 'we are already doing that!'

Remember one of the first steps in the planning of improvements is to realise how easy this can be rather than be daunted and build up an expectation of some huge programme being required

Getting yourself into the right mindset

We are all guilty of it: when we walk into the office we forget rather conveniently that we are all customers and we all have increasing expectations from the companies that service our requirements. We become the person that doesn't answer the phone even though we know it might be a customer (or sometimes because we think it is a customer!) because we are doing something else and don't wish to be disturbed; as managers we are often twice or more people removed from the real customer interface and those layers of insulation allow us to feign ignorance in terms of the consequences of decisions we may make or things we might do; we prioritise our personal or the company's needs over the customers without a thought until things start going wrong and customers begin to desert – then we scratch our heads and wonder what on earth could be wrong until the slow-dawning realisation that customers who are not looked after will slip away, often under cover of the night and without even having the courtesy to say 'goodbye'.

Yet you are probably among the most demanding and exacting when you are the customer – it is good to reflect on your own business for a moment and to think about the last time you tried out your experience and really thought about whether it meets the mark.

- Call the service desk with an imaginary complaint or query.
- Try and join schemes or just visit a frontline location and watch.
- Go to the call centre and do nothing but listen to calls for two days.

When we are customers we are constantly evaluating the service or effectiveness of the product we buy. In order to do this we are filtering a whole host of similar or adjacent experiences mostly unrelated to the product or service we may be interacting with, and we are constantly reappraising what is the norm and what is acceptable, what is better than acceptable and what is excellent.

The key point here is that we are using many different benchmarks. For instance, how quickly the best website pages refresh; how quickly the best broadband connection fires up; how in tune with me the best airline in-flight experience is; how good the best call centre experience is – these are the ever-improving tests being applied often unconsciously.

Critically reviewing what you are providing just using your own experiences will give you a strong indication of what your customers are thinking. Of course you are overlaying the positioning of your brand in that calculation, so if you are Singapore Airlines and renowned for world-beating service the expectation will be very different from a Southwest Airlines or easyJet flight. What this does show is that there is a direct link between the brand and the expectation and the service: if you set the bar low in terms of service frills because you offer the lowest price then customers will adapt and accept the logic; if, however, you are at the low-cost end and create an expectation through advertising that you are going to get high-end service then it is no surprise when customers complain.

Remember the old maxim of 'under promise and over deliver' is one that holds so true in today's world – build that thinking into your planning.

Aligning the leaders around the customer experience

For any customer experience activity to work you will need senior leaders engaged and active in support of the activity. The past has told us that well-meaning individuals in the mid to higher levels of management will only ever achieve limited success. In Chapter 11 we talk about the organisational challenges and how to overcome them. The challenges are often not about the general belief that improving the experience will be good for business but simply that leaders are not used to managing the customer agenda and are unsure what their role will be and how to deliver while managing their already busy diaries.

Share your plans with the senior leaders and then be clear about how they can actively support the activity and start to role model the customer-driven behaviours.

Your challenge is to show the leaders of the business that they can 'do this' without major disruption. Give them some simple tasks that will start to bring the team collectively closer to the customer.

For example:

- Spend two hours a month with frontline staff listening to calls.
- Discuss a prepared digest of customer voice feedback every week in team meetings.
- Visit a key customer with the brief to 'listen humbly' to what works and what does not work for them today – feed back what you learned.
- Be prepared to talk at a meeting about how your role impacts our customers.
- Add the top three customer complaints as a standing agenda item at board sessions – challenge individuals or small teams to manage improvements and report back on their findings.
- Add a question into one-to-one meetings with direct reports about the customer, e.g. 'next time we meet I would like you to have thought about what you do and how it impacts our customers'.
- Once we have identified where our role impacts on the customer 'identify one way to improve that experience'.

What you are doing is raising the profile of the customer as part of the business strategy but also starting to show support for the customer activity and promoting conversation about the subject.

The customer journey map

We now have the right frame of mind and two out of the three components of the plan to create the conditions to thrive – we know where we are, we know where we want to get to. We have begun to list down opportunities, but now we need a map of our experience from the customer viewpoint. What is required is that outside-in customer view of the end-to-end experience to act as a counter point and to complement the internal process maps. We need a customer journey map or CJM (we explore in detail how to create a CJM in Chapter 6).

The most common challenge at this point is we have lots of different customers who are dealt with differently, so how can we map all of their different experiences?

My experience from doing this across sectors, geographies and industries worldwide is that the reality is that as much as you might like to think you do, you don't actually. It would also be commercially crazy for most companies to have fundamentally different experiences. Every company has a backbone of infrastructure that has to work efficiently and we are all aware that building in complexity is expensive.

The simple answer is to map the experience that relates to the bulk of your customers and then down the track to create flavours of that core map that reflect different customer groups, e.g. business traveller versus economy.

What you will find is that there will be a few points during the experience where the experience varies and you can quickly map these out as variants on the core. For example, a high-value bank customer may be routed to the top of the queue in a call centre but they still largely get the same service when they are connected. It is these nuances that are important, as we will see when we work on the experience design.

During the mapping you will uncover additional opportunities for experience improvement that will add to your list from the internal document review.

Prioritising your opportunities

One thing is for certain: you will have more opportunities than time and resources to deliver them. So next you can take your list of all the opportunities, pull together a small team from across the business and consider which are the priority areas – and therefore the potential starting point for a deployment plan.

Remember one of the keys to success is some visible early wins that are delivered at low or no cost

A simple way to create a priority is to use an 'ease and feasibility' four-box matrix.

Along one axis we have feasibility using a simple scale of hard to very easy, and then on the other axis we have an impact assessment that reflects the impact on the customer, scaled from low to high.

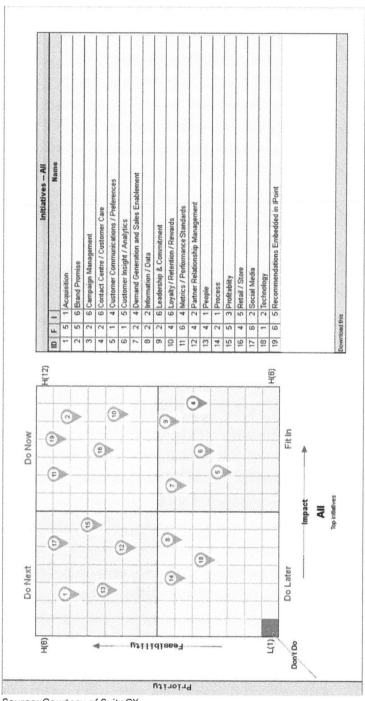

Initiatives -- All

ID	F	I	Name
1	5	1	Acquisition
2	5	6	Brand Promise
3	2	6	Campaign Management
4	2	6	Contact Centre / Customer Care
5	1	4	Customer Communications / Preferences
6	1	5	Customer Insight / Analytics
7	2	4	Demand Generation and Sales Enablement
8	2	2	Information / Data
9	2	6	Leadership & Commitment
10	4	6	Loyalty / Retention / Rewards
11	6	4	Metrics / Performance Standards
12	4	2	Partner Relationship Management
13	4	1	People
14	2	1	Process
15	5	3	Profitability
16	4	5	Retail / Store
17	6	2	Social Media
18	1	2	Technology
19	6	5	Recommendations Embedded in iPoint

Source: Courtesy of SuiteCX

Take each identified opportunity and using a sticky note place it on the chart at the appropriate spot – those that appear in the top right box will be the potential early wins as they will be easy to implement and have a high impact on the customer.

To make it easy to show visually in presentations later, apply a number to each opportunity and then you can use the number on the chart and provide an index to describe the opportunity.

Take the top right cluster and check to see if there are dependencies that will either cause issues or help you to sequence the initiatives.

Test the initiatives against your list of pre-existing customer experience projects inside the company – can they be injected into an existing team's work?

Consider if you can further prioritise into what you might call Nike 'just do it.' and those that might take some cross team cooperation or further work to deliver. For example, a simple change to words in a call centre script may fall into the first category, while a redesign of an on-boarding for new customers will take more planning.

Don't forget the other opportunities which you can build into the mid-term plan. So the next priority group that are high impact on the customer but harder to deliver will be bottom right; then bottom left and then top left.

Remember don't just plan for the short term, set out a plan over an extended time period

The dos and don'ts of creating your plan for experience change – think differently!

Your job now is to create a platform for change which others use and execute for you. Imagine you are one of a team of five maybe ten people in a company with thousands – how can you hope to drive change yourself? Besides, to assume you can is counterproductive as once people and teams assume you are doing it all they will switch off and work on other priorities.

Mass participation is the way to really drive change and evolve the culture simultaneously.

Remember you are working in the world of experience so think about how to make your customer activity fun, engaging, attractive and how to stand out from the other internal activity

- **Do** always look at what you are asking for from the other end of the telescope – you will find people much keener to help out if they see benefit for them either personally or their team. If you are perceived to just be adding workload for which no direct benefit accrues then you are going to find it harder to get the levels of cooperation you will need.
  - So think hard about how you communicate what you want and how you can evidence that this will have positive outcomes from your colleagues' perspectives.
- **Don't** expect big investments ahead of the 'return curve' but do gain senior team support for your plan.
- **Do** give the senior team a role to play – ensure that they are actively aware of the plan and give them opportunities to support deployment on a day-to-day basis as well as getting it on their meeting agendas and one-to-one meetings with direct reports at appropriate points.
- **Do** ensure that you are able to keep track of the changes and record them, creating a list over time – it is very easy to forget how things used to be.
  - Keeping a physical record of every change, however small, will allow you to provide a positive review each quarter showing the level of change.
- **Do** plan in how you are going to keep your CJM alive – how will it be used and how will it be visible in the business?
  - One example of how to do this is to carry a copy of the map around with you to meetings and when ideas are being discussed use it to ask where and how the plans will impact on the customer journey.

Remember the opportunity for positive exposure to the senior leadership can be a powerful persuader when it comes to supporting your plan

- **Do** try to avoid huge programme governance and overheads, by keeping your list of activities seemingly small scale, delivered quickly and then moving on to the next deliverable opportunity.
  - ♦ You should be able to minimise the 'programme police' interference, or as I sometimes called them rather unfairly the 'progress prevention' teams.
- **Do** spend the time to fall in love with the problem rather than rush to a solution – give yourself time to think differently and explore a range of possible solutions.
  - ♦ For example rather than redesign a piece of communication think about not using it at all or delivering it through a different medium or even at a different time.
- **Do** try using the hothouse approach when it comes to a more involved change, such as a CJM stage redesign.
  - ♦ Bring in a team of people from across the business for an intensive period of activity and then allow those resources to return to their day jobs, while you and your team refine their outputs. This has the advantage of being able to be pre-planned for calendars and it allows you to pull in a wider team to improve knowledge and communication that in turn will continue to have a culturally positive impact.
- **Do** set goals that can be measured and achieved weekly, monthly, quarterly that all add up over time.
  - ♦ Look to find existing measures and repurpose them as customer measures.
- **Do** push on open doors in the early stages.
  - ♦ You need the support of colleagues and time spent trying to persuade sceptics is both time-consuming and emotionally draining. Find open doors and push on those to create success and momentum

- **Do** look to use resources that are not necessarily already stretched – you will find that some key people seem to be in demand for every programme – they are almost too good at what they do.
  - ♦ Take the opportunity to give others air time – perhaps focus on a department that is not usually heavily engaged in non-core work activity, e.g. finance, or where there is a latent demand for activity in the customer experience space, e.g. the call centre.
- **Do** plan for periods of reflection at regular intervals (quarterly) where you showcase to the company the level of change achieved.
  - ♦ It is too easy to be caught up with the need to run faster, but the positive impact of looking back is underestimated. Build these review sessions into the plan, think about how you can present the information in an engaging way – perhaps a foyer display – plan to use meeting rooms to display customer experience information on walls, e.g. the CJM, and invite comments and questions, lists of changes, quotes from colleagues.

Remember the more that you can get people talking customer the better

Actively plan to engage the company

Your goal is to get the company using the word customer and talking about customers more and more. Use your social media; this is about subtly shifting the internal agenda. If senior leaders make statements about the customer experience make sure it is supported directly with evidence of what they will be doing visibly to encourage engagement. Customer experience has historically been dominated by 'sound bites' in the communication area, e.g. 'we are going to be passionate about our customers'. What is required, however, is evidence of how to:

- Create an online resource centre, particularly if the business is big and complicated and perhaps international – this way you can use the intranet to make information, tools, videos and other content available 24×7×365.

- ◆ You can load a virtual resource centre with a wide range of assets from 'how to' workshop guidelines to CJMs created by teams. It is particularly useful to act as a repository for team and individual 'stories' about their work and achievements in the customer experience space. Encourage teams to communicate with you about their stories of successes and their failures and publish these onto the intranet resource centre.

- Introduce internal rewards for contributions in the experience space – perhaps breakfast with the senior team to talk about exciting new ideas and how they can be implemented.

- As we have noted it is important to log all of the changes that actually happen as you go.

  - ◆ Create a list of the changes, however small, otherwise I can guarantee that you will forget a substantial number and when it comes to justifying the CE activity a lot of your positive evidence will be lost in the mists of time.

  - ◆ You will be surprised how much has been achieved so encourage others to tell you what they have done and when they have done it.

  - ◆ Plan in stages during your journey to take a time out and reflect and communicate what has changed.

- Include communication in your plan – how are you going to raise awareness of the activity and attract interest?

  - ◆ Create regular newsletter postings on internal systems like Yammer – let your imagination run riot to create an experience that will catch the attention of colleagues.

  - ◆ A formal communication plan is a good start point, however other more guerrilla tactics should supplement this.

  - ◆ Stimulate conversation by creating a digest of customer comments and circulating to a wide audience inside the company. You can create podcasts of customer calls from the call centre for colleagues to listen to on their journeys into and out of work.

Things to think about

The nature of customer experience is such that it does not fit neatly into a big programme plan box. Indeed to do so would limit its success.

You need to resist the situation where the customer is simply forced to adopt the company's preferred solution – explore your customer world and look at what could work for both customer and company.

Customer experiences are the outcome of a wide number of individual parts of the business working together to create an output called the experience, with those parts often owned by disparate parts of the company.

The plan is around creating a platform for the experience agenda to grow – it is about quick, short deployments that concentrate on volume of changes rather than the size of the programme. It is about finding ways to connect people and processes and getting the company involved in an active dialogue around the customer. It is about delivering on opportunities that have been identified using minimal resources wherever possible. It is about gradually raising the background awareness of the customer as a driver of business success and it is about helping colleagues to understand how their work contributes to that end experience. It is about creating, measuring and most importantly communicating successes over time.

The output of the plan is increased business and personal confidence in the delivery of customer experiences, and an increased understanding of the relevance of individual personal contributions to the customer experience that the company delivers.

6

How to use customer journey mapping

Customer journey mapping (CJM) is now becoming established as a standard component of customer programmes, but:

- What is the best methodology – how do you create maps quickly?
- How do you use what is in effect a customer treasure map and ensure that you actually have some 'Xs' that indicate where the treasure is buried in experience terms?
- What is the role of software to capture, share and manipulate maps?

Put simply, customer journey mapping is a structured way to understand and capture your customer's wants, needs and expectations *at each stage* of their experience with your company. Then to capture the individual interactions from the customer viewpoint from initial awareness to leave and perhaps return.

CJM is also a tool for visualising how customers interact with an organisation across multiple channels and touch-points at each stage of the customer life cycle (or part of it). It provides a factual basis for change, a map of the interactions that take place and the emotions created at each touch-point. The flipside of CJM is EJM (employee journey mapping) and we will look at the business and cultural value of developing an EJM for your business.

At the end of this chapter you will be able to: create a core 'outside-in' customer journey for your company; identify key interactions; begin to prioritise where and how to focus your resources on change; engage in creating an EJM.

Why is CJM important?

At its simplest a CJM is a mechanism to force the company to think like customers. It is a fact that while we are all customers in everyday life, when we walk into our day job we forget the customer and operate and think from the company perspective. For this reason the production of a CJM is an incredibly valuable way of bringing the customer back into the heart of the company's thinking – that said the process of producing a true 'outside-in' customer journey map will reinforce how 'inside-out thinking' dominates. It is often very difficult to sustain that external customer perspective without external and skilled facilitation; however, one tip is to ban the word 'we' from all discussions in CJM workshops. Inserting the words 'I the customer' will force the team to express themselves from a customer point of view.

Why create a CJM?

As we have identified, a CJM is a key component in your customer experience plan. It provides a current state view of the journey and then becomes a tool to:

- help you to plot out the changes you need to make;
- identify dependencies upstream and downstream;
- record changes to your experience;
- identify different experiences for different customer segments;
- communicate about the customer with your colleagues across the company; and with the help of software to
- aggregate data and information currently dispersed across the company into one location.

The actual visual of the map is highly valuable as it provides a simple nomenclature that you can use to ensure that all customer conversations are based around a common understanding.

This is very often the first time that an end-to-end journey has been captured. Businesses break up the ownership of a customer experience based on where the customer is in that journey and who is 'responsible' for them at that point: for example, during the awareness stage the customer is a marketing lead; then during the acquire stage, sales take over; then during 'welcome on board', customer services step in. It is a game of pass the parcel and in many cases the experiences are very different and the expectation, created by one group with a specific individual business measure or target in place, is not how it is delivered at the next stage. The creation of an end-to-end CJM allows you to ensure that you are aware of links and dependencies between different interactions along the end-to-end journey – it is a backdrop against which to review planned actions.

For example, in many companies regardless of their business vertical, sales tell the potential customer one story to achieve their target but the reality is different (software, for instance, is quick and easy to deploy and use but it is actually a highly complex deployment).

This is usually explained by a lack of alignment in performance metrics and is a very significant cause of the gap between customer expectation and customer experience reality, and the resulting customer behaviours that adversely impact the business results.

What is the difference between a customer journey map and a process map?

As we have described a CJM is an 'outside-in' view and is captured purely from the perspective of a customer. This means that we capture interactions that a customer has directly with your company AND interactions which the company may either have no or only indirect control over or visibility of. For example, when thinking about buying a new car you may well read magazines, reviews and often talk to people who will provide their own recommendation. This is all captured in a customer journey map – as it is a map of what we actually do as customers it would not be captured in a process map, which typically describes just the part played by a company seeking to supply the product or service to us, or what a company does to its customers.

Process maps also fail to capture the emotional context of an interaction, how a customer is feeling at that point in time, and what they expect and need from that interaction for it to be successful in their mind. Given that the way we feel impacts on what we do and how we behave, to be able to capture this aspect of the experience is critical to understanding why your customers make the choices and behave as they do.

So the value can be obtained in a number of ways, but the very capturing of the end-to-end touch-points can quickly highlight gaps in the company's coverage and experience.

One of the main reasons why companies do not actually produce true customer journey maps is because they believe that they already have a CJM only to discover that what they actually have are 'process maps' that describe from an inside-out perspective what they do to/for customers.

Get yourself a sponsor or don't start the CJM

The leaders responsible both at an executive and delivery level need to understand why they are asking the business or sponsoring a team to produce a customer journey map. It is imperative that they have a view on what they are going to do with it once it has been produced, and they need to be convinced that improving the customer experience leads to improvements in the business performance.

Experience has taught that without the buy-in and endorsement of the most senior executives, the likelihood of a programme being successful is considerably reduced if not neutralised. The impetus must come from the top of the organisation and then be sustained and monitored over time. Often the early impetus is there, but then as other priorities crowd in on time, the programme begins to stall through lack of focus. Often this happens at the stage where cost has been incurred but the benefits are yet to flow through – which gives an ideal window to postpone or stop the work at a critical point.

Remember, too many companies produce a customer journey map and stop there, believing the work is complete, but the reality is that first current state CJM is just an enabler of future activity

The message to well-meaning individuals in organisations is that they should accept the reality that their passion may not be rewarded unless the top team totally buy in to the philosophy. However, one learning which can help to get that leadership commitment is to focus hard on the fact that by addressing needs more effectively the experience is delivered more efficiently, reducing waste and delivering immediate opportunities for cost savings that do not damage the customer equity.

Setting an objective

Critical to the success of the CJM work is setting an objective from the outset. It is not acceptable to create a CJM just for the sake of creating it. The objective needs to be related directly to an in-year business issue. This provides immediate context and purpose for the creation of the map and provides the sponsor and delivery team with focus from day one. This is often described as the 'burning platform' that sparks the company into action.

This is why the pre-work outlined in the previous chapters is important in providing the insights to highlight early opportunities that the CJM work will enable.

Remember, do not start a customer journey map without understanding what business issue it is intended to focus on as an early deliverable

The initial objective needs to be deliverable within two to three months of commissioning the work, as maintaining momentum is vital for success. This is driven by the ability to show some early attributable business wins directly created by the CJM work – this may, for example, be: at a high level helping to deliver on the annual target for increased customer retention; at a more micro level it may be targeted to address failings in the current on-boarding of new customers that is causing concern both in qualitative and quantitative scorecards terms. This will also help where the team need to highlight a particular customer segment journey.

Who should create the CJM – picking the team

The production of a CJM is often the first 'set-piece' in a customer programme inside a company – as such it is a significant vehicle to promote and engage the different departments. When you are putting together a team to produce a CJM you are ideally looking for:

- 12–15 people drawn from across the business both vertically and horizontally – include a variety of levels and functions
  - ♦ we are looking to bring together different perspectives and to begin to showcase how both front and back office can contribute;
  - ♦ look to include finance, legal, compliance (where appropriate), sales, service, operations, IT, HR and marketing as a minimum.
- Influencers
  - ♦ we want these individuals to go back into the office and talk positively about their experience and to be creating engagement within their peer group.
- Motivated, engaged and vocal colleagues
  - ♦ customer experience work needs to be both energetic and engaging and the participants are key – so set up for success.
- A blend of youth and experience
  - ♦ we need a variety of customer viewpoints and voices in the room;
  - ♦ you are not looking for senior executives or board members at this stage beyond sponsoring input;
  - ♦ senior executives rarely have the day-to-day knowledge and their presence can be inhibiting for other team members. You can have them open and close the event but make sure they make clear why they are not attending in person. It is not because it is not a priority but because they could adversely impact on the team dynamic and inhibit some thinking as a result of their standing in the company hierarchy.

Being seen as a part of this team should be part of recognition wherever possible to create a positive feeling around attendance.

Remember part of the opportunity provided by a CJM creation workshop is to demonstrate to those who believe they are disconnected from the experience how they are actually pivotal

Getting started with your basic CJM

A CJM is basically composed of a customer life cycle divided into stages – that is, the 'backbone' of the journey and at each stage a series of interactions (often called touch-points) that the customer has.

When you first start to create a map it is good to begin at a very basic level and then refine the stages and descriptions as more detail is added.

Let's take a simple customer journey that we can all relate to and illustrate the steps to the creation of a more detailed CJM.

Creating a restaurant visit CJM

Level 1 – The 'heartbeat map'

This is so called because of the outline of the map that you will create. This is a technique I first saw being used by one of the more enlightened insurance businesses some 10 or more years ago.

All you need are four flip chart pages stuck to a wall side by side and a handful of sticky notes.

The challenge is to identify no more than four stages of the journey and name them using verbs to describe the stage. To do this you simply picture exactly what you would be doing as a customer and to assist the thinking you should create a scenario.

In this case the scenario is 'I am going to take my family out for a birthday celebration dinner'. Then write each stage out on a sticky note and place it at the top of each of the flip chart sheets in sequence.

Backbone life cycle stages: plan the meal; arrive at the restaurant; dine; pay and leave.

Life cycle stage	Plan dinner	Arrive	Dine	Pay & leave

Life cycle high-level stages

Having established the 'backbone' the next challenge is to identify up to four interactions per stage – the challenge of just four means that we will aggregate and avoid getting too detailed too quickly. Each interaction is described using a verb as they are actions and is written out on a sticky note and added under the appropriate life cycle stage, e.g. 'order food'.

Life cycle stage	Plan dinner	Arrive	Dine	Pay & leave
Interactions	Search internet	Park car	Order food	Ask for bill
	Talk to friends	Enter restaurant		Leave restaurant
	Call restaurant			

Life cycle and key interactions

Having completed this you should then draw a centre line from left to right horizontally across the flip chart pages – this represents the average expectation line. On the left side of the flip chart draw a vertical axis and label the top half 'Great' and the bottom half 'Poor'. This vertical axis is measuring the customer expectation of the individual interactions.

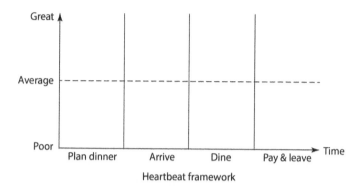

Heartbeat framework

Now we move all of the interaction sticky notes on to the centre line and in turn beginning with the left-hand side review each one by answering the question 'do I expect this interaction to be average, great or poor, or somewhere in between?' Move the sticky note to a position on which the team are agreed. Having completed this for each interaction, connect them using a marker pen.

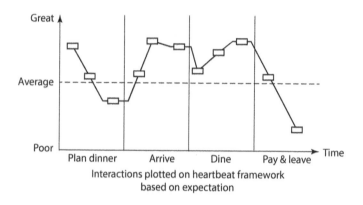

Interactions plotted on heartbeat framework
based on expectation

As you can see you have created a basic CJM which has already started to highlight that not each interaction we have has the same potential value or impact on the customer.

In this exercise you now ask one of the team to walk through an actual experience that they have had of this particular journey. If this was your business you can call on individual experiences and knowledge and other customer data, e.g. complaints, service levels, customer feedback. Using an X for each interaction you plot the actual experience and again connect the 'Xs'. What you will see are differences or gaps that can be both positive and negative between the expectation and the actual experience. Where they are below the expectation there is a problem, and where you are exceeding the expectation the question is whether that is positive or potentially an overinvestment in an area that the customer does not value that highly.

Finally you ask the team to highlight which of the interactions they believe have the potential to significantly influence the likelihood that the customer will return and or recommend the restaurant to friends.

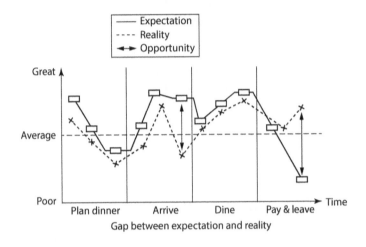

Gap between expectation and reality

Where there is a negative gap between the expectation and the actual experience and it is a key moment for the customer you have identified a key area to focus on improvement.

You can use this simple technique to look at business issues from a customer perspective and to begin to work out where to prioritise actions and effort.

Remember in CJM sessions insist on applying the test 'I the customer' and bar the word 'we' to help to think 'outside-in'

Level 2 – Journey maps

Having created a simple map and understood the challenge of thinking like a customer you are ready to progress to the next level of detail with your map.

Running a Level 2 CJM workshop

You need to allow at least one and ideally two days to create the first version of your core customer journey map. This requires organisation and cooperation to release the participants and is a useful early test of business commitment.

In preparation you need:

- ideally an external venue to take the team out of work mode thinking;
- dress down/casual – again to get the team into the mindset of a customer;
- a large space with clear walls that can be used to capture the journey;
- brown paper or flip chart paper to capture the outputs;
- sticky notes to capture individual interactions which can be moved around the journey if required and to signal different owners;
- a supply of marker pens;
- an enthusiastic and knowledgeable team!

As you worked through the Level 1 heartbeat map you will have identified a more detailed level of interaction even if it was not captured. With a Level 2 map we begin to expand the range of the journey map backbone stages and we will become more granular in the capturing of interactions – but following the same principles of 'outside-in' and using verbs to capture the interactions.

To help you, the following outlines a standard backbone that covers the end-to-end life cycle of a customer journey. This serves as the template for you to edit and adjust but will provide at least 80 per cent of the stages you will require. This template has been tested across industries, sectors and customer groups and has been validated as correct over many applications.

Explore	Aware	Select	On board	Use	Get service	Re-commit	Leave	Return

Example standard life cycle backbone

Test this standard backbone against your customer journey and where appropriate change the language but not the meaning of the stage, you also need to test to see if there are specific stages based on your company/sector that require their own stage. For example, in the insurance sector you would add a stage for 'Claim', in aviation you would add 'Flight', in credit cards you would add 'Collections', or in a software business you may have 'Technical Support'.

Remember, to qualify as an additional stage in a customer journey it must be a significant part of the customer experience unique to your company/ sector. You should not exceed 12 stages in a journey backbone

In the example we are using of the restaurant visit, the enhanced backbone would look like this:

Explore	Aware	Select	Book	Arrive	Dine	Pay	Leave	Return

Restaurant enhanced backbone

Having established the 'backbone' of the journey the next task is to take each stage and step though a simple set of tasks.

Stage by stage in sequence, establish the needs of the customer at each stage in the journey.

Beginning with the simple prefix 'I need . . . ' we capture the needs of the customer at each stage of the journey – these are a mixture of both tangible and emotional needs, so for example at the point of purchase, the customer may 'need to be reassured that they have made the right choice', while at a more functional level they may 'need to find the nearest restaurant'. The more needs gathered the better as these will help when the experience is reviewed and a more granular approach to a particular inter-action is carried out. They are captured as short narrative sen-tences in the first person, such as 'I need to ask friends what they think'.

Capturing customer needs

So in the case of our restaurant visit we may capture the following as examples of needs in the 'arrive' stage:

- I need to be recognised.
- I need to feel welcomed (warmly).
- I need to know that the cake we ordered is here (discreetly).
- I need the table to be ready.
- I need the table I asked for.

Enhanced interactions

Next, stage by stage in sequence define the high-level interactions that a customer will have.

An interaction captures the customer connecting with someone or something as they carry out an activity. The activity may or may not be with the company as this map captures the experience from the customer perspective. So, for example, 'talk to friends' or 'read magazine' are often interactions when seeking advice – these will be captured but this is not controlled by the company. As such they would never appear in an internal process map but they are important aspects of the customer journey. Exploring the above example further, the company is able to look at this jour-ney and if during the aware stage it becomes clear that presence in key influencing magazine titles is critical to getting into a potential customer's 'consideration set' then the questions that follow are: 'do we have a presence?' 'if not, why not?' and 'if yes, is it good enough?'

The wording of an interaction is important – it should be brief and wherever possible contain a verb as it is capturing an action, such as 'negotiate contract', 'receive documents', 'research on internet'. This third example also picks up the channel that a customer is using and each channel used by a customer should be specified where appropriate: for example, 'call restaurant for booking'. The acid test is can you insert the description 'I' in front of your description?

The level of granularity of the initial map is also important and 'high level' is the first stage to achieve – for example in an automotive map example the details behind 'take a test drive' can be expanded significantly at a later stage if that is determined as a critical interaction from the customer value perspective, but that is sufficient detail for a high-level core map.

The approach is to take each stage of the journey and walk that experience from a customer perspective and write on sticky notes the interactions that happen – at this point, sequencing is helpful but not critical and the best approach is to brainstorm the experience and capture all the ideas that are are then aggregated and filtered. Each stage has the interactions laid out below it and once completed the team review the sequence and reorder the interactions into a logical sequence.

Grid format customer journey map

Alternative grid layout by channel

Source: Courtesy of SuiteCX

Remember when you first generate the core map you do not need to consider the timeframe for the individual interactions – in reality some interactions may follow each other in minutes, others may be months or more apart

Once all of the stages are complete you will have the core of a Level 2 map. This will already begin to reveal facts about the current experience. For example, how many company-owned interactions happen at each stage, which shows where most of the effort is today in terms of the experience you deliver. If the majority of the interactions are in the early stages of the journey then it is clear that most activity is around acquiring customers.

The next step is to revisit each of the interactions and ask:

- Do we have or own this interaction (e.g. if the interaction is 'read magazine' during the 'aware' stage do you have a presence)?
- Who inside the company is responsible for that interaction (noting that some interactions are owned by the customer, e.g. talk to friends)?
- Where there are multiple teams involved you must decide who has lead responsibility?

As you make the decisions, create a list of each department and assign it an icon for use later – this can be as simple as the m for marketing. Once you have assigned all the interactions across the map you will be able to create a simple icon-coded version and supporting 'legend' that details the department by icon. Once you have an icon-coded version you will be able to see at a glance where the ownership of the experience lies at different points in the journey. Where there are multiple icons in the same stage you have an opportunity for breakdowns, handoffs or duplication in the customer experience as it is highly likely that the customer is being handed off to other departments: for example, during 'on board' the handovers may be between marketing, sales, customer services, operations, finance and legal!

The finished product records the key stages of the journey in sequence and the key interactions that a customer could undertake as a part of that journey. At this stage the only reference to time is in the natural sequencing of the different stages. There are then different ways to present this visually to the company. It is a good idea to find out how the key members of your audience think – so a grid pattern appeals to logical thinkers, engineers, finance and technical people but the marketing and service teams may need a more visually appealing presentation.

This is an example that shows a different visual journey format.

An alternative visual representation of a CJM

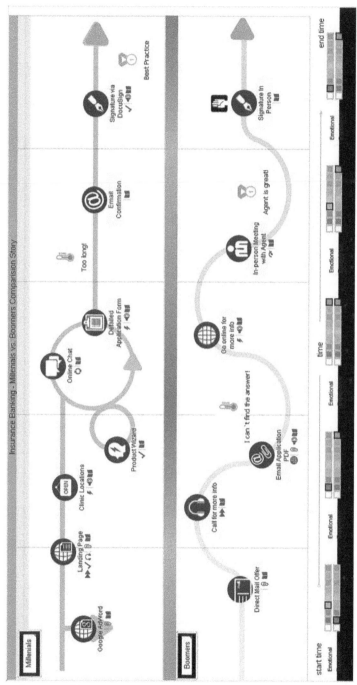

Source: Courtesy of SuiteCX

More visual representations may appeal to more visual learners and you can use shaded icons to highlight particular components of the experience.

Example of icons

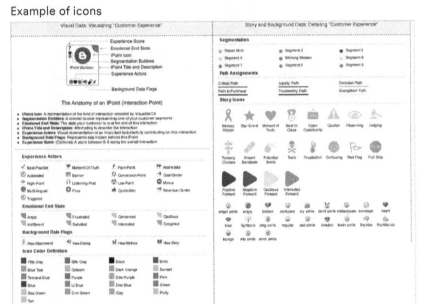

Source: Courtesy of SuiteCX

Remember the structure of a CJM helps the company to understand the customer journey and what is important to customers on their journey

Now we have a core CJM and we can begin to carry out some first line diagnostics on that map.

Take the detailed needs that the team identified for each stage of the journey and consider whether the experience as mapped that your company delivers through the detailed interactions actually delivers against those customer needs: if not, identify and record gaps in the experience. This is a quick test and is designed to identify if there are significant gaps in the 'as is' experience.

For example, if customers need to be able to order online and the experience you deliver misses this interaction then you have an issue and an opportunity that is impacting on the business commercially.

Remember a key output of the initial CJM evaluation is a description of current state and some early opportunities for change

Stage-by-stage capture known issues/ opportunities and then prioritise

Next the team goes back over each stage and identifies known and new opportunities and issues from the customer's perspective and these are recorded – these challenges will help to provide input into the prioritisation of next stage activity in terms of improvements and experience design changes. This is the first time that the team is allowed to use information from the company perspective, in this case to highlight known issues and opportunities in the existing experience. These should be captured in simple descriptive/ narrative format.

Prioritising your interventions

There are a few ways that you can now look to prioritise your lists of opportunities and issues. At a very simple level where opportunities and issues align you have a simple potential priority.

Having collated the opportunities and issues, you can, as outlined in Chapter 5, then plot these on to an 'ease and feasibility' four-box matrix – one for the opportunities and one for the issues. For simplicity of capturing the positioning of each opportunity/issue on the matrix assign each one a number. The team then comes to a consensus agreement on the position against the two axes using a simple high/low scale which can be graduated 1–10 for the impact, and a similar scale for the feasibility where you are assessing the ease of implementing a change to realise the opportunity or resolve the issue. The result will be a simple scoring and ranking of the list of opportunities with those in the top right-hand box being the early wins for the team to focus and act on.

Remember opportunities or issues do not only need to be at an individual interaction level – they can be at a group of interactions level or a life cycle stage, e.g. on-boarding

An alternative way to prioritise is to understand firstly those interactions that are touched by most customers – not every interaction will be relevant to every customer segment. This involves agreeing your key customer segments, understanding the persona that you developed (the pen picture of your customer) and the needs of those customer segments, and then walking the map from right to left highlighting those touch-points that they interact with. Having highlighted the common interactions, check to see where the opportunities and issues align against those interactions. The point of convergence will give you a potentially high-impact intervention opportunity when measured in terms of numbers of customers.

My preference is to use the ease and feasibility matrix as the start-off prioritisation – this keeps the process simple and does not involve the need, for example, to create multiple personas or to generate detailed interaction variations that occur based on the customer segment at this early stage.

The challenge at this point is to get into action quickly and effectively, not to engage in too much detailed background work that will slow down deployment and lower confidence levels internally that you will deliver positive change.

Creating variants on the base map

Companies do have different segments of customers and they may vary the experience based on the particular segment. For example, a restaurant may have loyal, repeat customers, VIPs, business customers or other distinct groups. Each of these segments may have some experiential variations. These may be the same interaction delivered differently, for example greeting on arrival, or may be additional interactions, such as valet parking.

To map these variations the team with the knowledge of the customer segment takes the baseline map and validates the experience for that particular segment, making changes, adding, deleting and in time documenting the experience for that specific customer. In most cases there will be a high degree of overlap between the base interactions with nuances of experience details being the main differentiator.

Remember there will be cases where the customers have the same interaction point but their specific experience of that interaction may vary – e.g. the variation between economy and business travellers at airline check-in, security, lounge, boarding the plane, travel, collecting luggage

Developing the segment-specific CJM at the next stage means you can capture variations in the 'how'. It is important to keep in mind that having too many experience variables can create confusion for both customer and company and is often an unnecessary cost for the company.

Getting granular – take a section of the map and explode the detail

Having established an area of focus the next step is to create a more detailed and granular map of that sub-section.

The approach to creating the more detailed sub map is the same as for the core map but you are able to get into more detail. For example with the restaurant you may choose the 'at table' component and start to get into the detail such as seated at the table, waiter introduces themselves, specials are explained, wine order is taken, starter is delivered and so on.

Creating mini maps – capturing the planned and unplanned interactions

Once you have your more granular stage level of detail you can create mini maps that take into account the duration of an experience. This recognises that not all interactions or touch-points happen at the same time – while several interactions can happen within minutes of each other some may be separated by several days or even weeks. You need to capture both planned and unplanned interactions with unplanned activity being customer driven, and often the result of an experience failing, plus the actual sequence of the interactions.

So in the restaurant visit, an example of an unplanned activity might be to ask where drinks are, chase up food order or complain about food.

Although an individual can do this, it is recommended that you set up a workshop with a wider team – using this as another engagement opportunity; it can be completed in less than half a day.

The set up for the workshop requires:

- the list of interactions written out on sticky notes;
- flip-chart paper on a wall;
- spare sticky notes for new interactions to be captured;
- the team needs to agree the scope of the mini map – for example, the 'in-restaurant experience' and the appropriate timeline, minutes, hours, days, weeks or months. Create the timeline increments on the horizontal axis, which in our restaurant example would be 15-minute slots over a two-hour period (the average time spent in a restaurant);
- take each of the sticky notes and place it into the correct sequence in the correct timeslot – you are mapping the customer reality at this point and it is important to be honest about this. In the case of the restaurant, what is the real wait time between arriving and placing an order? Once all of the

interactions have been placed on the map the team should check that there are no interactions missing – and where they are, add them in;

- look at the 'white space' (that is the gaps between experiences over time) and ask yourself, is this ok? Or do we need to intervene in experience terms? So, for example, if the wait time for food exceeds 15 minutes, do we need to give the customer an update?

Think about how it feels if you are expecting something to happen and it doesn't. You could be waiting for a train or be a passenger when a flight is delayed on the runway. Receiving no information on the reason for the delay and the likely duration raises stress levels after only a few minutes – the benefit from updates even with limited information is it reduces the need for your imagination to fill the gap and to raise your stress levels. So do think about the impact of white space – is it fine to leave a customer applying for a loan several days without updating on the status?

Now take each interaction in turn and ask the question: 'is this a planned interaction or an unplanned interaction?' For example, checking where my order is would be an unplanned interaction initiated by a customer concerned about wait time.

You now have a view of the interactions over time, the duration, planned and unplanned contact and can easily identify any dependencies across the timeline.

For instance, as we noted in the restaurant example, delivering food in a timely manner is connected to taking of the original order – do we wait for the customer to complain or deliberately design in an intervention in the case of delay?

Remember that experiences can be over in minutes or extend over weeks before they are concluded

All of these stages provide the baseline map that can then be used to redesign existing experience, or design a new experience that better delivers the customer experience.

Should we buy software – what do we need software to do?

As you will have now seen there are layers to the creation of customer journey maps – each stage takes the map to the next level of detail. Each version of the map can be created in basic tools such as Microsoft PowerPoint or Excel.

In the short term a couple of key advantages to using an established but simple software tool are that it acts as a reminder of the process, the data you can and could capture and it professionalises your outputs.

Additionally, if you want to create different versions of maps, including variations off the same base for different customer segments and eventually progress to using the maps to aid redesign and change management then software is a sensible option.

As you progress with your customer activity the software option allows you to gradually build out in a very structured and common format, eventually gathering and collating the customer experience data and information from their dispersed locations across the company.

For companies that operate in regulated space, from utilities to financial services, the ability to demonstrate your approach to customer experience strategies is significantly enhanced by this consolidated approach.

Remember you can present the customer journey in a variety of different formats to tell the story – think about what will work best for your audience

When considering the software solution you do need to avoid the mistakes of the CRM system purchases where the buyer was often seduced by the art of the possible in terms of the capabilities that are embedded.

My analogy on buying this type of software is to take the 'Excel test' where most of the users of that tool probably use less than 10 per cent of its true capability. Be an informed buyer: understand what you are actually going to use your software to do and where that capability extends the current capability inside your company.

For example, the customer experience software will have project planning tools embedded but you will already have an internal tool and approach for that. What you are buying is more about the structures, the thinking and logic that ensures that you have a prompt to remind you what you need, and that you are able to capture what you need then to be able to access, use and generate useful outputs and visuals. I see the software as a way of collecting and ordering the key pieces of information and data – it is in reality a repository for your information, *it is not the business solution*. Here are some ideas as inputs into your software decision:

- It should enable you to share and collaborate across the departments and geographies.
- It should be flexible enough to offer a range of visual treatments.
- It needs to be easy and quick to use with an intuitive user interface.
- It needs to have sufficient depth to capture further details at an interaction level – e.g. training guides, measures, ownership, emotions, etc.
- It needs to interface with your current IT and add value to the infrastructure.
- It needs to be affordable and scalable – able to grow as your competence and need grow.
- It needs to have been developed by customer experience professionals who understand how you will use it.

Remember all of the systems have an enterprise capability, but you are likely to only use a small percentage of the overall capability. Priority needs to be focused on usability and fit for purpose rather than a long list of what it could do if ever required

In terms of which system to choose, the recommendation is to focus on those that have been built by actual practitioners where the tools have been built to meet the known need. Most of the large software vendors now claim to have CJM and customer experience systems, but in my view they are more about the features, benefits and functionality than the practicality of use.

Things to think about

Commonly asked questions

What does journey mapping involve?

As you will have noted from the restaurant visit example, the actual CJM building is very structured. The bigger question is how much time should we spend on creating a CJM? In the early days of the CJM story we used to take anything up to 8–12 weeks to step through the process, but today there are short cuts. Today you can create maps in two to four weeks. Then allow up to four weeks to validate your map and opportunities with internal colleagues and real customers.

The benefit of taking longer is that you can engage a wider group of people in discussion prior to creating the actual map. The downside is that a CJM is in the first instance a retrospective view of what you do today – it is at worst just an artefact, a static picture and investing too much time in its creation risks loss of momentum. It also risks sponsors asking the question 'so what?'

At the other extreme, given the increasing maturity of journey mapping you can buy an off-the-shelf map for your sector or vertical, after all virtually every bank, telco or airline core experience is the same when seen from the customers' viewpoint. Once obtained it is a relatively quick task to validate and adjust for your specific company.

The answer lies between the two because the unwritten upside of 'creating' a CJM is the opportunity to engage colleagues and gain ownership of the map, while moving quickly enough to satisfy the true need of the company; that is, not to create a pretty picture, but to start to introduce change and show improvements. So the use of a clever skeleton map which is sufficiently formed in the mind of the facilitation team will accelerate the work, as will pre-preparation around the identification of customer needs to act as prompts, as outlined in this chapter.

So the CJM is the foundation, the backdrop for the future changes and it should not be undervalued in terms of the wider cultural issues that customer change poses.

Remember you can accelerate the CJM production but balance this against the value of ownership of the outputs and the opportunity to engage a wide cross section of the company

We have lots of different customer groups so which segment do I choose? (You may think you deliver unique experiences but you don't really deliver on them.)

One of the first and most common challenges when embarking on a CJM exercise is defining who the customer is. This may seem very basic but it is key. It is very common to have companies saying that they are unique in the world of the customer, and that they have multiple customer journeys all of which are different and tailored to the different customer segments that they have identified.

At this early stage it is key to keep things simple (KISS – Keep It Simple, Stupid). The reality is that while there may be 'flavours' of different journeys there will be a core journey that applies, and if you think about it that makes commercial and business sense. Most companies have a common back office and systems infrastructure and to optimise the efficiency they need to have common processes. The idea that you are going to create a wide range of bespoke journeys does not make sense at either level.

▶

An airline passenger still needs to check-in whether they are economy or business class: the physical touch-point is a check-in desk, the nuance of the service experience is the only differentiation. So the CJM component at the high level is the same and the detail for a business traveller can be captured as a variant on the core journey.

The simple rule is to look for where the highest volume of customers transact and map that core journey, or use the CJM approach to attack the biggest opportunity or risk you have identified in the early planning stages, using that to define the customer group impacted. Having created that core journey you can then take different customer segments, and using the base map validate and amend where necessary. What you often find is that the variations are not as extensive as you actually believed, which is a telling finding in itself. As an example, the difference in 'customer' experience between retail and business banking is less than the different teams often want to believe. You need to open an account, you need access to cards, you may need to arrange an overdraft, and so on – this may be conducted in a different location and you may have a business manager rather than a bank manager, but from a customer perspective it is not really that different. In one such test I discovered just four additional interactions!

Remember start with the biggest customer group to create your first core map – then use that as a base to create variants for different customer groups over time

Why do we not go straight to customers to create a map?

Of course this is possible, but it misses a fundamental opportunity to engage the colleagues in the business first and to gain that ownership. At the next stage the map they have created is taken out to customers to validate, and it is fun to bring back an updated map to those that created the first version – in true Pareto terms they tend to be 80 per cent right!

Can we group customer journey stages?

It is possible to connect different stages into logical groups – so, for example, the early stages of explore, aware, select could be collectively seen as 'customer consideration', or use, get service and recommit could be 'experience engagement'.

Remember the steps to creating your first outside-in CJM: high level, simple KISS – it is very easy to get too detailed too quickly. Remember you can get really detailed once you focus in on key areas of your journey that you want to improve

How should you validate the CJM – external customer research?

Once the internal CJM is produced and has been internally validated by a cross-functional team, you can take the outputs out to external research. This is not essential but is often seen as a need by companies in order to further build in confidence in the conclusions. I would recommend that you push for this where you feel you need to use customer input to challenge internal assumptions that you feel are impacting negatively on choices.

The best way to do this is to use a series of focus groups that you either manage yourself or use an external agency to manage. The objectives are to ensure that the CJM is an accurate reflection of the actual customer experiences, to highlight gaps and add in interactions. The second purpose is to highlight the critical interactions from the customer viewpoint and develop a prioritised view on issues or opportunities to improve, alongside areas where the company performs well.

▶

What you will almost always certainly discover is that the customer has a slightly different view to the company, both on the actual experiences and the key priorities.

Remember the best way to validate is to get your focus groups to step them through the CJM spine, not the individual interactions. Get them to tell you their experiences through stories and then extract the information, rather than walk through the CJM step by step

How do you test a CJM against the stated business strategy?

Having created the core journey map it is relatively simple to test the overarching business strategy against the map by highlighting interactions on your map. This is made even easier if you have adopted a software platform that allows you to filter the core map and create different views.

If, for example, the key strategy is retention, you go through each of the interactions and highlight those that are directly contributing to customer retention. While it could be argued that every interaction in some way contributes to the customer's view and therefore likelihood to renew, you need to ask a more direct question – 'which interactions are direct contributors to assist us to achieve our stated business goal of x% renewal rate this year?' This test is of a higher order and can expose some uncomfortable truths about the investment in experiential terms in the business strategy. To create a starker image you can remove all of the interactions that are not directly contributing – to emphasise the issues further simply provide a count of the number of interactions left versus the total number of interactions in the core map.

If you feel too uncomfortable with this approach you can highlight those interactions that you consider to be critically important to a customer's likelihood to renew, and then ask how well you are performing at those points in the customer journey.

To add weight to your internal view on which interactions are most important you can research data sources inside the company – these could be as simple as checking in with frontline staff on current key complaints or using internally available research on complaints and positive feedback (the positive can be equally as revealing as this represents a positive action by a customer to recognise something they have clearly seen as important).

How do you map current customer-badged projects against the key customer interactions?

As we have seen, companies will have ongoing initiatives designed to improve customer experiences – we have listed these at an earlier stage of your planning.

You can look at the objectives of the customer projects and align them with the CJM. What can emerge is that several 'activities' are focused on one interaction; this needs to be coordinated to ensure that customer impacts are connected.

Remember just because an activity is already in flight you should not assume that you could drop an idea – it may be that value can be accelerated through the new opportunity

Case study

'Nedbank: how we use our CJMs to improve decision making'

Introduction

Nedbank Group is one of South Africa's largest banks and is a JSE Top 40 company with a market capitalisation of R119.5 billion (as at 30 June 2015). Old Mutual plc is the majority shareholder with a 55.4 per cent ownership of the bank. The group's main market remains South Africa but has presence in six other African countries and an approximate 20 per cent shareholding in Ecobank Transnational Incorporated (ETI), enabling a unique one-bank experience to clients across the largest banking network in Africa, comprising more than 2,000 branches in 39 countries.

Nedbank Group offers a wide range of wholesale and retail banking services and a growing insurance, asset management and wealth management offering through frontline clusters: Nedbank Corporate and Investment Banking, Nedbank Retail and Business Banking, Nedbank Wealth and the Rest of Africa Division.

The challenge

The Nedbank Group's positioning, which has been in place for more than 12 years, defines Nedbank's distinctiveness as being great at listening, understanding clients' needs and delivering. In 2006, the bank set itself the challenge to become a world-class service organisation and created a strategy to achieve this objective. The strategy was reviewed annually using a customer management diagnostic and benchmarking tool, and 5–10 of the top recommendations from this assessment were prioritised, allocating executive accountability for their delivery. Over the years these recommendations have provided the impetus for the continuing evolution of the client-centred strategy. Various projects were implemented as a result of the annual assessment: including a highly successful service proposition 'Ask Once', creating excellence in complaints handling, and launching a social media centre that received acknowledgement in the *Harvard Business Review*.

In 2012, the executive made the decision to communicate the client-centred strategy to all staff through café sessions (sit-down discussions) that ran for a full year. By the end of that year every staff member understood that the client was at the centre of everything the bank does, and the level of understanding of the strategy remains high and consistent to this day. The choice of the word client as opposed to customer in a retail environment was also strategic to drive relationship building.

In 2013, having a relatively mature client-centred strategy that was well understood, Nedbank adopted *client journey mapping* as a tool to design all future innovation and change. Although journey mapping had been used in the business previously, it had not been fully integrated into all parts of the business. In 2013 the client experience intent was defined with the involvement of the executive team. It created a platform to deliver the brand promise. This was augmented by *client experience principles* derived from client insights. Nedbank had already at this point progressed significantly client segmentation research and personas had been created for each client segment. These insights were therefore used in collaboration with focus groups to validate an outside-in approach of the client journey.

The business then went ahead to adopt these client experience intents and principles to drive business change and innovation. All projects are assessed using client experience as a lens in addition to financial value and speed to market. Client journey maps have been created for key moments of truth (MoT) and these evolve as new insights are created. Client journey maps then guide changes in processes and systems and ensure a consistent experience that delivers to client expectations.

Key to the delivery of the client experience is continuous alignment of the organisational culture. Culture was identified as the key enabler to delivering the right client experience. Many initiatives exist in the organisation to drive a client-centred culture including definition and measurement of ideal behaviours, learning and development programmes focused on client experience as well as ongoing service recognition. Annually an executive immersion programme allows senior members of staff to visit the client-facing businesses, including the branch network and contact centres. The objective of the programme is not only for executives to show their support to the staff, but to also hear and experience first-hand what happens on the ground from both staff and clients. The executives are encouraged to draw from these insights in their business decision making.

▶

While client journey maps are a great tool to understand the client's experience at key moments of truth and then design the ideal state, on their own they cannot transform an organisation. For real transformation, 'client' must be at the centre of the strategy that needs to be role modelled by the organisation's leadership team. A good understanding of the client is also important and therefore segmentation and creating personas is a precursor to designing the client experience. Nedbank uses the journey maps to inform process mapping and system design, but the people deliver the client experience. Nedbank has also embedded measurements at different levels, operational, tactical and strategic, and these measures drive synchronised decision making at all levels. Over the last three years the NPS (Net Promoter Score) has steadily improved from 11 per cent to 21 per cent, showing the success of this holistic approach.

Employee journey mapping

The other side of the customer coin is the employee and this component remains critical to success. What is the role of individuals in creating a culture that gives employees every opportunity to engage with the customer and to ensure that the customer agenda is integrated into the day-to-day rhythm of company life in a seamless way? Ask yourself these questions:

- How well do you connect all of your employees to the end customer?
- Do you have an employee proposition?
- Does your culture encourage customer focus?

Unlike customer journey mapping (CJM) that has become widely adopted as an approach and tool when working on customer experience, the employee journey map (EJM) has not been widely adopted and is in its infancy as an approach. Yet in my view the employee journey is just the other side of the customer journey.

If staff are not engaged then the customer experience is likely at best to be sub-optimised.

The simple approach of creating an EJM and then driving improvements is a great way to engage the wider company and to support the cultural shift that may be required in order to allow the company to engage more effectively with the customer and the customer experience.

It is for this reason that the EJM is a tool that you can use to underpin your customer experience work and to ensure that you have the best possible conditions for customer experience improvements to deliver real differences.

The process of creating an EJM mirrors CJM – but of course in this case the customer is the employee.

What is the purpose of employee journey mapping?

At the macro level the EJM looks at the relationship between a company and its staff – it is used to highlight the sweet spots in the employee journey where employee engagement levels can be raised to drive real customer value. It is also about understanding how improved employee engagement with both the customer and the company will lead to greater advocacy of both the company as a place to work and its products or services. This can be translated into the word 'pride' both in the company and its products or services.

The primary purpose in creating an EJM in this customer experience context is to establish those sweet spots where injecting a strong customer component to the employee interactions can be directly connected to improvements in the customer experience and customer outcomes.

For example, does your induction process focus on the importance of the customer to everyone in the company, or does it prioritise on health and safety, and administrative rules?

The secondary but important business benefit is that you will have created an end-to-end view of the employee life cycle, and other areas of general improvement will emerge that will contribute further to improved employee engagement.

If we created a simple model of how this then translates into an improved bottom line, it looks like this:

Employee engagement = better customer experience delivery = customer advocacy = job satisfaction/ pride = lower staff churn = employee advocacy of company and service/ product = business growth = business bottom line improves

The commercial reader will ask how much do I need to invest to get the return? The answer, rather like the wider customer experience, is often very little – you are simply adjusting existing approaches, processes, content and more.

As you develop an EJM and you look at the opportunities for change that are highlighted you will look at three dimensions:

- the formal journey: induction, personal development plans, performance management, training;
- the informal journey: team meetings, away days, one to ones;
- environmental aspects: office, IT, corporate culture.

The first two are captured in a single EJM, while the environmental dimension is an overlay that gives context to the map.

Getting started – do you have an employee proposition?

- The first question is do you have an employee proposition? Check with human resources as your first option!
- Most companies have a customer value proposition, but quite a lot do not have a clearly articulated employee proposition against which they can hold themselves and their employees to account. The employee proposition can give real insight into what working for a company should be like and how that aligns with the customer promise or proposition. It should act

as a signal to those considering joining the company and provide a reason for those already on-board to stay.

- Your customer proposition should in effect be a two-way contract that highlights what you will do for the employee and in return what the employee will do for the company – you call it a pact or a contract. Take the brilliant example below that comes from a Virgin company some years ago that very effectively sums up the culture.

'It's not easy to sum up our culture in just a few words. For starters, we're such a fast-moving, complex business that change is a constant feature of our operation. Every one of our people has to have the intelligence to think on their feet and respond to any new developments that come their way. All the while, of course, they'll be working hard to deliver the unique brand of service for which we are renowned.

This, in turn, creates a lively, collaborative environment where everyone knows what's expected of him or her and works together to achieve it. In fact, we pride ourselves on being as honest and unpretentious as we are inspired and professional. Everyone has a chance to voice their opinions and no one's too proud to ask questions, which only serves to increase the inclusive nature of our culture.

Similarly, we embrace innovation, wherever it comes from. So if someone – be they employee or customer – has a brain-wave, we'll listen. And if we like it, we'll do it. It's another way in which our people are the driving force behind our success.

Of course, it takes a certain sort of person to flourish in such a fast-paced, free-thinking environment. Talented, self-motivated, enthusiastic, you'll have to share in our passion for providing only the very best. Put people like this together, and you create a winning performance culture that thrives on inspirational leadership, positive attitudes and commercial flair.'

If you don't have an employee proposition create one – you can use the following prompts to help.

- An employee proposition is a 'promise' from an organisation to existing and potential employees that:
  - ♦ is consistent with the organisation's brand;
  - ♦ is distinct from the employee propositions of competitor organisations;

♦ is credible in that it echoes the actual experience of current employees;

♦ is relevant and valuable to both existing and potential employees;

♦ is honest and not a stereotypical or clichéd statement.

The employee proposition provides a reference point for future changes to the employee experience.

Can I do employee journey mapping without an employee proposition?

Of course the answer is yes, in the same way that you can do CJM work without describing the experience you want to deliver – but it makes it harder to test your planned solutions. Additionally it makes sense to take the opportunity to at least start to create an employee proposition, as this is another piece of the customer experience jigsaw that you can create.

Who should lead on employee journey mapping?

The customer experience team can lead on the methodology and approach, but as this is about the internal employee experience you should embrace a wide range of functions and levels. Once again engaging a wide cross-section and significant numbers of your colleagues will drive the success.

- Find a sponsor – from a senior executive level you will usually find that the human resources director will take a lead.

- Provide the sponsor with a short brief and a précis communication of the reason for the work. As an example you could say:

'As HR sponsors and leaders we are focused on increasing employee engagement as a lever to increase employee advocacy. In order to understand what matters most to our employees we need to be clear on the key things that will have the biggest impact to drive up engagement. Currently we have shopping lists of issues and initiatives with little direct understanding of the impact they drive. Learning from work done in mapping our customer journeys where we have identified our customer priorities we now need a

complementary approach to mapping our employee journey to ensure we apply the same rigour to our own employees as we are to our customers.'

- Capture through an audit the existing in-flight or planned activities, projects and programmes that are focused on employee engagement.

The principles to adopt and business benefits

The principles of an EJM provide the touchstones for the team as they engage with the work.

The following set out some of the principles an EJM can include:

- create a visual and itemised end-to-end employee journey capturing stages of the journey and specific interactions between the company and employees;
- understand the real drivers of engagement and to do it in a way that takes you a long way from the traditional but often hackneyed and not actionable annual survey;
- provide employee voice to offer an outside-in view of the experience, including how it feels to be an employee;
- agree to follow up and make changes to the employee experience by operationalising recommendations;

The following set out some of the benefits an EJM can provide:

- identifying current performance shortfalls;
- prioritising change where it really matters for employees;
- challenging existing activities to improve return on investments;
- creating a common language and framework to manage the future employee experience.

If you use the principles or develop your own and achieve the benefits, you will improve employee engagement, improve advocacy of the company as an employer, and improve employee advocacy of your products and or services.

Things to think about

Exploring how you create opportunities to improve employee engagement with customers and the company and connecting this to the resulting customer experience is a very constructive way to look at how to begin to alter the culture of the company. There are many opportunities during the regular working day to reinforce the messaging and they are neither expensive nor difficult to execute.

The following set out some of the aims of an EJM:

- providing a common framework and language to engage with the employee experience;
- improving engagement just through the creation process;
- improving the employee experience and engagement;
- identifying quick wins and more strategic change opportunities;
- contributing to culture change;
- connecting the external customer journey to the employee;
- bringing the employee voice to the table without the need for a sterile survey.

As with the CJM and customer experience change, of which this is a contributor to the cultural change part, the mantra is *hundreds of tiny changes completed by many different people to make a difference*. If every one-to-one meeting in the company has a customer component, that alone will have an impact. Likewise, if every personal development plan has a customer engagement and connecting component, or if every team meeting begins with a customer story whether about your own or another company's experience, the cumulative effect is to raise the consciousness of the end customer across the company and improve the engagement of the employee with your company.

7

How to design new and improved experiences

The new area of growth in customer experience is the design and redesign of customer-driven experiences – what framework exists to help teams to truly deliver changed and improved experiences? Using examples I will illustrate how teams can really innovate and drive improvements using expert facilitation and structures to support them. We will also consider the issue of 'wow' experiences and provide examples of how they can be deliberately built (experience by design) rather than be the response to failure, as is so often the case. Let's explore the answers to these questions:

- How can you move from ideas into action by integrating outside-in thinking with the inside-out processes of the company?
- How do you truly innovate and design experiences that meet your customer expectations?
- How can you learn to think differently?

We have seen that by applying the tools and approaches in the earlier chapters that you can emerge with a prioritised list of improvement opportunities. The next challenge is to take opportunities that identify weaknesses in the experience and redesign those experiences to improve the customer experience and the customer outcome. This applies both to redesigning an existing experience or designing a completely new experience – for example, for a new product or service or perhaps a digital execution.

This is not about process re-engineering – that may be an outcome but it is not the driver – nor is it about Six Sigma or Lean process. This is about deliberately designing an experience that is optimal for the customer from the outside in.

At this stage it is critical that thinking is not constrained, and that means ignoring what might be seen as limitations on what is possible.

The ability to think differently relies on the freedom to reimagine how an experience can be delivered, including if it even needs to be delivered at all!

You start with a blank sheet of paper and begin by considering whether this needs to exist. If you confirm that it does you then look at how it can be delivered.

Part of the problem of doing this without some external facilitation is that you are sub-consciously constrained before you even begin – for example you will find people who at the outset consider their personal time to be fully allocated and see little point in adding something new that cannot be delivered. Others will simply say we have done this before and it didn't work – it is easier for an external person to say perhaps what you did last time was wrong than it can be for an internal person.

The ability to think differently and challenge the status quo is one of the hardest tasks for a team or individual inside an established business. I would suggest that for this specific work around innovating and thinking differently, you need some external help – as your confidence grows you can then take on future workshops in-house. As I have said to many clients over the years, the last thing you need is a lot of people who think like me inside your company – at certain points, however, that thinking is critical to the customer experience work you do.

As an example of thinking differently, I am embarking on a global campaign to change airport arrivals. Over the years I have arrived at various airports around the world, often weary after many hours of travel, usually entering a new environment and just wanting to get out of the airport and to my hotel to chill out and relax. Sadly I have accumulated many frustrating hours trying to find my taxi drivers – I know he is one of the grey-suited faces holding a hand-written sign with my name on it but there are hundreds to choose from. The walk of shame when you have made a first unsuccessful sweep is stressful and by the second rerun the emotions are boiling over. This is happening as you read this book – it is happening at hundreds of airports every second of every day. Why? Because that is the way we do things, the smart ones even use an iPad now with the name in black and white on the screen – how technology has advanced this particular experience!

The solution is to think differently about this and view it from a customer perspective – in effect repurpose the question.

Q. What do I need?

A. To be able to find my taxi driver (an individual I don't know) as quickly as possible *in a crowd.*

Q. How do you stand out from a crowd so that I can spot you?

A. Do something different to the other 150 taxi drivers.

Q. What can I do to stand out?

A. Hold a single balloon in the air, or if you have an iPad turn the screen bright orange – no need for misspelt names just the visual sign.

I tried this simple change on a colleague coming into O.R. Tambo International Airport, Johannesburg, who had to navigate its very busy concourse with all the grey suits and signs. She saw it even as she came through the doors, went straight over and was on her way within seconds. How did she feel? Relieved, not stressed, perhaps even happy! Check out the visual cues on the next page.

The cynic says, 'what if people adopted this and there were five white balloons?' Well, the law of averages says I will get it in three and that is already better. The reality is that anything can be used as a visual signal in a crowded environment, from a banana to a funny hat. Can you imagine how much more fun airport arrivals would be, not to mention colourful. Of course, from a business perspective it works too as you are reducing the frustration and extended wait time of a driver, and if you're a hotel you are extending the hotel experience into the airport!

Just ask your taxi company to do it and we can change the way that this operates in thousands of airports around the world, impacting positively on hundreds of millions of experiences. This is an example of thinking differently and challenging the accepted norms in a way that costs nothing to implement yet has a tangible impact on customer experiences both rationally and emotionally. It is also

Even a different shape can stand out - spot the circle!

Source: Kumar Sriskandan/Alamy Stock Image

An easy way to stand out in a crowd, even in black and white!

Source: ImageBROKER/Alamy Stock Image

about recognising that significant experiential improvements can be achieved quickly, easily and without incurring huge costs or making big investments – customer experience is about being agile and continuously improving.

What we are looking to do is to highlight particular stages or inter-actions from your analysis of the customer journey where there are opportunities to improve and where we know there is a high poten-tial to influence the customer by at least meeting, and preferably exceeding, their expectations at that point. Having done this you need to apply structure and an approach that will produce an enhanced and potentially differentiated experience. Once we have defined that design, the business inside-out approach will be brought into play to work out feasibility, the necessary changes and to create an implementation plan.

Think about how difficult it was to execute the change to an inter-nal process for the circular sign experience and the negligible cost.

Remember that visual non-verbal cues can be powerful when designing experiences

Are these wow moments?

Let's take a moment to reflect on the issue of creating what are commonly called 'wow' moments. How many companies say we want to 'wow our customers'? The definition of wow for me is something completely unexpected and something that signifi-cantly exceeds your expectations. The reality is that most wow moments are a product of failure somewhere else in the company that drives an individual to go to an extreme to recover this. We will all have examples of where that has been the case – for exam-ple, the insurance claims person who, having found that a family would be stranded and miss their holiday, hired a car for them with their own money! We are never quite sure if the stories are true or get embellished but we get the picture. It would make no commer-cial sense for companies to continually wow their customers except through their unfailing consistency in delivery of their experience.

Think about it: something that is a wow one minute can quickly become the expected norm once we all hear about it.

My advice is that you can design in wow moments but they need to be very carefully timed and specific – they are often free to deliver, but are more about the timing than the cost of the experience.

Remember once you understand how to purposefully design experiences you can apply the same principles at a micro level without the need for big set piece sessions. Add it to your armoury of approaches to solving business issues and developing business solutions

Preparing to design

The process is: to collate inputs – run your experience improvement workshop – validate the outputs with customers – refine the ideas – engage with the internal processes to ensure that the changes can be deployed.

You need to engage in some convergent thinking that is pulling together a range of materials and creating some further inputs ready for an experience improvement workshop.

As inputs you have, as highlighted by your earlier work:

- your customer journey map
- your design guide
- your problem statement or opportunity.

You need to produce a design synopsis that details the considerations for the team that should include:

1. What the opportunity is – e.g. the scale, the competitive advantage created.

2. Where you are today – e.g. summary of the drivers for the change.

3. Other factors to consider – e.g. metrics, data/technology influences.

4. The design session plan – e.g. who is needed? For how long? What is the timeline?

To ensure that your workshop and its outputs are going to have real value to the business bottom line, consider as part of your design synopsis what the business benefits will be, what business relevant issues you will be addressing with your outputs – for example, improved conversion rates, better engagement, reduced cost to serve.

As additional inputs to the workshop stage you can put together a couple of documents that will act as a team brief around the actual experience if it already exists, or as a projection if you are engaged in a new build. This is an opportunity to bring the emotional content into play.

Next create your persona, or personas if you are considering more than one customer group that have different needs. As outlined earlier, you should focus on painting a picture of this person and their lifestyle so that the team can take on that persona.

One tip is to get a range of magazines and cut out images that you feel bring the persona to life – such as holidays, cars, house, make-up, fashion and so on. This is like producing a mood board when doing internal decorating and can be used as stimulus during the workshop.

Second, create a small template and detail out the customer's needs at the rational level; then a section on the customer's emotional needs; what outcome does the customer want; detail from your CJM the key interactions; detail who is involved in the delivery of the experience both front of house and behind the scenes; and do not forget those business benefits.

Finally collect any supporting collateral, including copies of marketing material, letters and other collateral that relate to the interaction today.

This material will be used as reference material by the design workshop team and also as stimulus material.

Preparing the design team

You should select a group of colleagues from across the departments and functions – for the design workshop you can have as many as 20–30 people involved. Just ensure that you have the right ratio of facilitators to participants – I would recommend a 1:10 ratio as the maximum to be comfortable that the workshop is effectively facilitated.

When choosing your team, look to involve different levels and ask your colleagues to select people that are worthy of recognition – this should be seen as a very positive role to be selected for. You also need people that will be willing to contribute in a group environment. This will be a two-day workshop and will require commitment for the entire time with little access to work and other priorities.

Remember that everyone in the design workshop needs to have an equal voice – make sure they do and that the experience is truly liberating

Find a venue that is preferably out of the workplace to avoid distractions; ideally this will be an overnight stay in a hotel to encourage work into the evening and then over dinner. Many good ideas emerge and you will be giving the teams some homework to do while they are at the workshop!

Once you have the team, you need to prepare them for the workshop – you need to get the team into the mindset of being customers. One way to do this is to encourage them to engage in an experience before the workshop and make notes on what they expected the experience to be like and what actually happened, picking up on what was good, what was bad and what might have been better. They need to base their feedback on the gaps between what they expected and what actually happened, and importantly think about how it made them feel.

Ask your participants to send in their thoughts and findings at least one week before the workshop, you then review the findings and create a digest for discussion at the event. The digest should look at where the experiences met or failed to meet their expectations, the emotions that they felt and what triggered them to feel that way, design ideas and lessons learned.

Here is a draft email that you could use to introduce the participant to the event.

Dear James,

As you will now know from your team leader you have been selected to take part in our upcoming experience improvement workshop focused on improving the way we introduce new customers into our company. We are both delighted and excited to have you as part of this cross company team. More details will follow shortly but in the meantime we would like to invite you to send us some feedback on an experience of your choice – it could be a meal out or a shopping trip, it's entirely up to you. Before you go, think about and write down what you are expecting it to be like and how you expect to feel, and then let us know how that compared with what happened: what were the highs and lows, how well did it meet your expectations? Please send your completed experience notes back to us by 15th March.

Thanks and we look forward to welcoming you later this month in person!

The idea is to get the team to engage directly as a customer and to think about elements of that experience that they may not normally even think about.

Engage a visual artist for the workshop afternoon of day one and then day two – this is an approach I first saw used by the brilliant N'Lighten team in South Africa. The opportunity to bring ideas to life real time visually adds a huge amount to the experience.

Confirm to the participants the outline for the two days and that the dress code is casual – we want the team to feel relaxed and informal.

If you want to really give the team an experience, connect with the hotel and ask if you can arrange two different check-in experiences: one where the experience is good, the room is ready, the service is prompt; the other where the reservation can't be found, the room isn't ready and then when it is the bed is not made – use your imagination! During the session you can ask the team what they think of the hotel, and of course we will see very different responses before you reveal that this is all a set up to show how experiences drive emotions.

The experience improvement workshop

The first stage is to prepare the rooms for your participants; you will need a main room and then breakout rooms to accommodate the teams. Teams of six are a good choice – that allows enough breadth of knowledge and not too many that people's voices are not heard.

Remember to mix up groups to provide different viewpoints and do not be afraid to change them during the workshop if the dynamic or knowledge sets are not working

This is the time to encourage divergent thinking so decorate the walls with enlargements of the design guide, the collateral, the personas, the business challenge and area that you are all going to design, and have the material in smaller scale available on each team's table as reference material. If you are having more than one persona then you will need to allocate the personas to different teams – for example, VIP guest versus casual diner in the restaurant example.

You can prepare an agenda that lays out the steps but do not put timings on the sessions – this leads to expectations and you need flexibility to adjust as the time progresses. The only given is that you need to have designed a new experience by the close of day two. The skill of the facilitators is key here to ensure that you get the best possible outputs.

Get the team to begin to list down initially in groups and then in plenary the messages that the company is trying to convey and the messages that the customer is trying to hear. List these on sticky notes on the wall. You will find that there are often more messages than you had expected! The teams now have an additional piece of collateral for their design – how do we communicate these messages and when?

Remember make the workshop environment fun and stimulating, use videos to highlight wow experiences, make sure there are sweets and props for people to use, take frequent breaks

Now initially as a big team you can ask for early thoughts and ideas on the interactions you are discussing and designing. You can make this initial discussion more structured by asking the same question in different ways: for example, 'what could we do for free?' or 'if we had £5,000 what would you spend it on to improve the experience?' The idea is to get big ideas out on the table again to feed into the smaller group discussions.

Remember the sessions should be two-way and involve discussion – encourage the team to contribute rather than just broadcasting

You are now ready to get into the detail of design by breaking into groups. If you have different personas, ask the teams to be in the mindset of that persona. If you have a single persona then you have two choices. If the interaction is big enough to be broken into two parts with a natural divide, you can brief teams to look at the different stages, or you can have all your teams work on the same interaction/s. In either case it is great to get different takes on the same brief.

Remember to include all of the senses when you design – you can put up flip chart sheets to remind the teams to consider: sound, smell, sight, touch and in some cases even taste.

You may be thinking to yourself, 'are all of the senses really important?' The answer is yes! Think about your sense of smell and how that connects you directly to memories: perhaps new mown grass, or fresh bread. Hotels use a signature scent to connect customers to previous visits. Think about how a song coming on can immediately transport you back to a specific memory – it is these subtle additions to experiences that can have a significant impact.

If you have an overnight in a hotel, challenge the individuals to think about a new idea that the company could consider as a way of improving the customer experience – in this case do not constrain their thinking to the task in hand but to any aspect of the company's experience where they see an opportunity. Start day two by getting the teams to collate their ideas on sticky notes, then stick them on the wall and have the teams review them and identify the best three ideas. This is some added value for the company and customer experience team.

The group design brief

What?

Design an experience that:

- is ideal for your persona;
- builds on your varied and collective work and experiences to date;
- is not constrained by anything;
- brings to life your experience and design brief and guide.

How?

- Create a design for the experience you are reviewing (a mini ideal state CJM map in effect) that records what is happening at each key moment, and records your customer functional needs, the emotional needs and outcomes, and detail how the redesigned interaction will address pain, where the critical points are, show where the messages will occur, and how.

- Generate new ideas and challenge everything from the need to do this to the channel used, and have you considered all of the senses?

- For example, the sense of smell as we have noted is a strong driver of memories – if you visit the upmarket Aesop boutiques and buy their products they are given to you in a reusable cloth bag (eco-friendly) and the bag is spritzed with their signature scent to remind you of them. The design workshop is about attention to detail as well as generating the big idea.

- Incorporate the messages that you have highlighted where you feel they are appropriate.

- Create a narrative that tells the story of the experience in the customer's own words, including how they feel.

Here is an example of how you might write a narrative in customer language that describes that ideal experience, including a focus on the emotional state of mind and how the customer is feeling as they step through the experience. In this example you are sending a gift using a delivery service:

'So I now want to send my gift. I've clicked the gift delivery button and it's given me some choices: Register as a Guest or Open an Account. They both have simple explanations under each of the boxes telling me what each one means. Signing up for an account sounds a little bit too involved and will take me longer. I'm going to sign up as a guest. So I'll select 'Send as a Guest'. I am expecting this to be really, really, quick and easy like it is on other sites where I have done this. The next screen is asking me for my name and then my email address and a password – it has a box next to it telling me why they need it and what they won't do with it like selling my information, sending me loads of offers I don't want, so I am relaxed about sharing my address. That is it, 'job done' and I have a simple but nice message 'Hi Alan a very warm welcome to the MET Gift Store. You are now a registered guest and you can send gifts at any time by entering your email address and password when prompted at the log-in screen. We are delighted that you have chosen to join us and just to say thanks here is a special service just for you – if you would like us to include a handwritten note with your gift just enter the details here! Now just click here to give us the other information we need to send your gift.

That has easily met and maybe exceeded my expectations – really quick, I didn't need to use the help button and a nice human response with a special offer to use right away!

- Create a visual version of your experience design using your visual artist.
- You also need to show what will need to change 'under the water' to make this interaction brilliant and unique – this means identifying the tools required to equip those involved, considering if metrics need to change and what training would be needed.

Be prepared to feed back in detail to the group, highlighting how you approached the task, what your ideas are and what your recommendations are.

Remember to check how well the design ideas incorporate the messages that you have identified that the customer needs to hear and understand

This design stage should take up the afternoon of day one and all of day two allowing for around 20 minutes for each group at the end of day two to feed back.

Remember that external facilitation can be really helpful to avoid you dropping into a very company-constrained way of thinking and to keep up what I would describe as a crazy pace and energy level that forces ideas out

Feeding back

This is an opportunity for the teams to use their imagination on how best to feed back their ideas to the group and to get across their new experience. Don't be constrained. I have seen teams create mini plays and acted out the new experience, some have created a cartoon-based visual experience, others even created dummy collateral.

Remember take lots of photos of the event, you can record simple interviews with participants talking about their ideas and the session. This brings the event to life for those you might be presenting to later

As each team has fed back their ideas to the group give the audience the opportunity to identify ideas or thoughts that they either like, love or want to steal. Get the audience to put their marks by those highlighted ideas: a simple tick for like, heart shape for love and the word STEAL speaks for itself. This gives a quick insight into how the ideas have been received – if you want to steal an idea it means you could use that straight away to make a positive change tomorrow.

The outputs

The customer experience team takes the outputs of the workshop and consolidates these into a report on the opportunities and ideas – you can also create a composite narrative that draws on the individual group work to describe in words the new customer experience complete with visual illustrations. The opportunities are broken into immediate 'just do it', and then a proposed hierarchy based on ease and impact analysis.

You may feel confident enough at this point to take the ideas to the sponsors and move into deployment. Many companies will insist on external validation to underwrite the ideas. This is easy to execute: you need to run a series of customer focus groups and take them through the key ideas, including the visuals as stimulus. You will emerge with a customer view on what will work and a potential priority to then feed into the sponsor sessions.

Inside out meets outside in

Once you have the approved set of ideas and your new designed experience, the final stage before deployment is to engage with the inside-out business processes.

You are asking the question: 'what do we need to do to make this happen?'

Remember it may be that you have some staging posts in terms of the delivery of the new design that get you there in a series of steps. This approach is preferable where there would be a long delay to implement the full experience

At this point you need to assemble the right internal resources dependent on the needs of the design – this may include process, data, technology, legal. The point is to get the right players into the room to create the business solution to deliver on the experience. It is at this point that there is a risk that the experience will be significantly diluted – your challenge is to stay true to the principles of the new design and to look for compromise only where it makes overwhelming commercial sense. Even when you need to compromise you should be looking for alternative ways to deliver the same customer outcome in experience terms as the driver.

Next, agree a set of measures to provide proof points that the changes are delivering measurable improvements in the customer experience and to the business bottom line. See Chapter 8 for some pointers on how to approach this.

Things to think about

What company in its right mind would allow its experience to happen either by accident or based on whoever is delivering it and how they feel that day? Answer: far, far too many today. Do you?

Experience design is about thinking about and potentially using all of the senses, and you should not be afraid to think about significant change. Ask yourself simple questions:

- Do we even need this to happen at all?
- Should it be a different channel?
- How could it look, feel and be different?

There is a space for incremental change but do not think of design in experience terms as just reworking what already exists.

When you challenge norms, how often will you hear in response to the question 'why do you do that?' – 'because we have always done it this way', as if that makes it ok!

Design is about deliberately choosing to design an experience from the outside in and *only then* engaging with the internal process of how to deliver. This is 360 degrees away from the current way that experiences are designed, if they are designed at all.

The principle is to think differently and to use the opportunity to challenge the accepted norms.

- For example, if a person died in military service would you really need to see a formal death certificate before you paid out an insurance policy?

▶

- For example, why do the best people in an estate agent in the UK work during the week 9 a.m.–5 p.m. when potential buyers need them at the weekend and in the evening?

It is by challenging what we accept as the norm that you will truly create new and differentiated customer experiences that can change the way we think and see the world.

8

How to use measures to drive and deliver your experience

This chapter will look at some of the key metrics being used today and will consider the right mix. We will also look at how to repurpose existing measures so that they are seen as customer measures. The real challenge is not to add in new measures to companies that are, very likely, already measured to death. We will look at how to focus on the handful of measures that really count and which drive actions. This is linked to the need to have flexibility and fluidity in the view of key measures over a trading year:

- What customer measures exist?
- How do you make customer measures relevant deep into your business?
- How can you repurpose existing measures?

Customer experience and the balanced scorecard

The good news is the customer is already most likely a key part in your company measurement framework in the balanced scorecard. For those unfamiliar with this term, according to Investopedia it is 'a performance metric used in strategic management to identify and improve various internal functions and their resulting external outcomes. The balanced scorecard attempts to measure and provide feedback to organisations in order to assist in implementing strategies and objectives.' There are usually four components of a balanced scorecard: Financial (Financial Performance); Process (Efficiency); Organisational Capacity (Knowledge and Innovation); and Customer (Satisfaction).

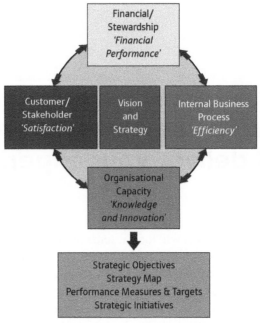

Adapted from Robert S. Kaplan and David P. Norton, "Using the Balanced Scorecard as a Strategic Management System," Harvard Business Review (January-February 1996): 76.

The bad news is that companies tend to focus on three out of the four elements of the balanced scorecard and emphasis is skewed away from the customer component, which is the least understood and believed by many to be the least quantifiable.

All too often the thing missing from your business strategies is input from the customer and a clear link to meeting needs and delivering noticeable benefits to them.

Instead the focus is on what such a strategy will do to benefit the business, usually in terms of sales or business efficiency – while these may be entirely appropriate measures, they need to be part of a set within a balanced scorecard.

For example, the way in which companies measure the success of their customer service teams, which is typically on the speed with which they answer a call, implicit in this choice is the assumption that this is of primary importance to the customer. In reality it is rarely the most important to the customer but is a convenient measure for companies in terms of internal efficiencies, time management, incentives and a range of others – it is much harder to measure first time resolution to the microsecond. These measures are driven by a mix of accounting rigour and 'internal intuition', which assumes that customers think the same as those working inside the business – again this is rarely true and means the need to really understand your customers by talking to them is neatly circumvented by staff becoming a cheap and 'effective' proxy for real life.

Evidence is freely available which demonstrates a gap between what the company *thinks* is important to customers and what customers *actually* deem to be the most important when it comes to making their choices. The failure to understand what is really important leads to customers receiving a sub-optimal experience and the company sub-optimising its commercial position.

Measuring up: where do you start?

The area of customer measures has been the focus of much corporate attention over recent years as businesses grapple with the problem of how to measure their new-found enthusiasm for all things customer.

Start with a review of what your company measures today both quantitative and qualitative, initially focus on those that are badged as or seen as customer measures inside the company. Make a simple list and then find out who manages the measure and who acts on the information provided. Compare the number of measures that are customer versus those that are 'other' to get a feel for the relative importance.

Remember what you will probably find is that this task is not as easy as it sounds and you may struggle to identify specific customer measures. That is a finding in itself if your mini audit comes to that conclusion

How you measure customer experience success presents a challenge, especially to companies that have a long-established set of business measures. It is critical to provide measures that align with your required behaviours and focus at each level and functional unit of the business – measures drive behaviours.

This principle does not mean abandoning high-level measures for personal ones or hard measures in favour of a basket of soft qualitative customer measures – it can mean being inventive in terms of what is measured or the focus given.

In many cases no new measures are needed initially, but rather the flexibility to change the area of focus to reflect the business need. A particular measure may require focus for a few months before it is replaced with another as the objective is achieved; in other words, dialling up and down on a range of measures. It also requires the ability to translate the corporate measures through the business in a way that reinforces the end customer impact as a key metric for all.

In markets where the scope for growth through customer or competitor acquisition is limited, the retention and development of the existing customer base becomes a strategic imperative. In pursuit of delivering a competitive experience, most businesses routinely measure customer satisfaction. This can be very beneficial in identifying and targeting specific problems and enabling teams to be targeted and held responsible for change. Attaining high satisfaction is a competitive prerequisite. Satisfaction measures, however, are less useful in helping businesses to establish the change agenda required to drive growth as there is limited correlation between customer satisfaction, loyalty and business growth – typically a high percentage of defectors are satisfied or highly satisfied with their previous suppliers.

Customer loyalty is regarded as a key driver of performance. Studies show that companies with above average customer loyalty index scores have price–earnings (P/E) ratios that are more than double those of their competitors. Companies with loyal customers and employees enjoy higher margins and greater profits than those that fail to retain and satisfy their customers. Obtaining growth requires companies to go beyond customer satisfaction and create an experience that results in customers trusting the company for its consistent delivery of promises, products, services or solutions. Knowing what makes customers loyal and the degree of loyalty felt is essential if increased value is to be realised.

Remember that measuring customer satisfaction alone is not enough

Where customer satisfaction is important

Customer satisfaction measures a customer's 'rational' perception of the company against their expectations of a specific product or service experience. It is a practical measure, ideal for identifying and targeting specific problems and enabling teams to be targeted and held responsible for change.

Most major companies measure customer satisfaction in some form and see it as a valuable way to assess a customer's experience of the interactions between the customer and the different parts of the organisation.

Customer satisfaction measures provide valuable insight, particularly where assessments are carried out by segment or value group – however, you do need to ensure that the vital opinions of the most profitable customers are not lost in the 'averaging' of the whole base.

The customer satisfaction risks

Think about the following as you assess the reliability and value of your customer satisfaction measure:

- How current are your questions, or are they largely a fixed set of questions (to allow tracking), possibly not reflective of the current customer world?
- How has your relative performance moved over time?
- How timely is the information? Many of the studies are undertaken on an annual or biannual basis. The completion and analysis can take several weeks and in the case of large surveys even months before the results are communicated throughout a business.
- How actionable is the information?
- What has changed as a result of findings from your survey?
- What is your annual investment and what is the return on that investment?

Even the most satisfied customers can defect

Achieving customer satisfaction may be an essential requirement to compete but a satisfied or even very satisfied customer will often defect where they are not committed to the brand – 'I'm happy with your product, but I'm just as happy buying another brand.'

Satisfaction results rarely predict or even correlate with repeat-purchase behaviour. In B2B markets, studies have shown that up to 65–85 per cent of defectors were satisfied or very satisfied with their former supplier.

Customers may be considered increasingly promiscuous, and attaining their loyalty can be a very difficult task, so the challenge is to provide a customer experience that successfully differentiates the organisation and drives brand loyalty.

Satisfaction measures are less useful in helping businesses to establish the change agenda required to drive growth due to the lack of correlation between satisfaction and growth. Actions taken to improve satisfaction may not feed through to be reflected in business growth.

To illustrate the point that customer satisfaction indexes (CSI) can be hugely misleading as a result of these factors, we need only review the impact of the comparison or competitive experience set via which we make value judgements. For example, when Virgin Atlantic launched its upper-class airline service and captured swathes of previously loyal and highly satisfied British Airways first-class passengers.

In effect what British Airways first-class passengers were satisfied with was what they knew about the service relative to other current competitive airline offerings, then Virgin changed the rules of the game – cars to the airport, quick check-in, bars, lounges, massages, etc. The CSI results were instantly rendered redundant as a customer measure, given it was viewed as a proxy for loyalty. The simple logic that had prevailed was that very satisfied customers are de facto loyal and unlikely to defect.

Another example would be the world of hotels where traditionally satisfaction surveys have been as much a part of the fixtures and fittings in a hotel room as the bed.

As every business traveller knows, they can expect to see a survey left on the bed and included as part of the checkout documentation and a quick survey reveals that the questions being asked are predictable too. This seems to match an enduring view about what is important to us as customers: how was check-in? was the bed comfortable? is checkout efficient?

In reality in three- to five-star hotels these have become hygiene factors – what is of real importance to the business traveller in particular tends not to be measured. For example, how easy it is to access the internet; how good technical help desk facilities are; or at a personal level it can be as simple as whether fresh milk is available for tea and coffee – given all rooms have a fridge it may be infinitely preferable to UHT sachets.

The point here is that beyond the hygiene factors there are a range of more detailed issues, which will actually be the ones that make the difference between a future booking being made or the recruitment of a loyal customer. These issues remain undetected because of the in-room presence of a standard CSI form, which is assumed to do the job when in reality it is a 'hygiene' check that relates to the minimum table stakes required to be competitive in today's market. It may be that front of house managers should spend more time listening 'naively' to customers to hear what little things will crank up loyalty.

Remember that customer loyalty is a proven driver of business performance

Understanding what drives customer loyalty is an essential first step

Leading customer experience organisations regard the level of customer loyalty as a critical indicator of future success.

A customer's loyalty is derived from a combination of functional and emotional experiences with the brand. To achieve high loyalty, as a minimum, the customer must be satisfied, see the product or service as important and perceive competitors as not providing the same or better.

To achieve loyalty, product and operations managers need to understand what it is that makes their customers *committed* to their product, service and brand. Understanding what drives loyalty is key as it has a clear and proven link with business performance.

Remember that loyal customers are more profitable – increasing the value of existing customers and reducing the acquisition cost of new customers

Companies with satisfied, loyal customers enjoy higher margins, greater profits – and consequently higher P/E multiples – than businesses that fail to retain and satisfy their customers.

As we have already noted, studies show that companies with above average customer loyalty index scores had P/E ratios that were more than double those of their competitors.

A customer's value rises with increased loyalty as:

- acquisition costs are amortised over a longer period;
- there is a tendency to increase their purchases and percentage of spend;
- they cost less to administer;
- they refer others, act as evangelists, spreading good news across markets;
- they are willing to pay a premium;
- they tend to forgive mistakes or underperformance in the product.

Customer experience measures

Let's take a moment to consider some of the commonly talked about customer experience related measures.

As outlined above, the premise underpinning the effective measurement of the customer experience outcome is often seen as an assessment of customer loyalty, how a customer feels about a brand, and the understanding that the strength of feeling expressed is a reliable indicator of future behaviour.

Different questions have been tested over time to assess which best predicts future growth. The question with the highest relationship to growth is 'would you recommend us?' Satisfaction has a weaker correlation with growth prospects.

The willingness of an individual to make a recommendation to a friend or colleague is recognised as the best indicator of loyalty as they put their own reputation on the line. It requires a strong emotional commitment.

Recommendation is a more 'instinctive' customer measure than satisfaction. It encompasses multiple experiences of a company, as well as more emotive issues. This appears to be why it is indicative of longer-term behaviour.

As the customer experience discipline has matured more work has been undertaken to create measures that help to connect the experience to the company business results. Over the past few years a number of bespoke customer-driven measures have emerged, including Net Promoter Score (NPS), customer/client effort and customer expectation.

Net Promoter Score

Of these measures the NPS has been the most widely adopted. The depth of the evidence to support the connection between an NPS score and business performance has been seen as compelling.

First introduced by Fred Reichheld in the 2003 *Harvard Business Review* article 'The One Number You Need To Grow', this distillation and ability to focus hard on a single data point is attractive to business leaders.

Net Promoter Score relies on a single question and work by Fred Reichheld, Bain & Company and Satmetrix has shown, with empirical evidence, the answer to which correlates to improvements in business performance – an attractive proposition indeed, and one whose siren call is increasingly answered by very substantial businesses.

Put simply, the measure asks customers to say 'how likely they are to recommend your company to a friend or colleague' using a scale of 1–10 where scores of 0–6 are labelled as detractors, responses of 7–8 are labelled as neutral and responses of 9–10 are promoters. By taking the percentage of the scores between detractors and subtracting that from the percentage of promoters you derive the Net Promoter Score or NPS.

The supporting research showed a strong correlation between propensity to recommend and future loyalty and impact on business performance over time. This measure now appears on senior managers' and executives' key performance indicators and personal KPIs with a note writ large to 'improve this score at all costs'.

The question for you if you are deploying this measure and the business has a strategy to improve the direction of travel of that score is: 'How do we operationalise this in order to effect the required improvement?'

In short the answer is to ask the qualitative free text supplementary question 'why did you give this score?' to give context and a quantitative overlay. This information provides the context for the customer response and reveals to you what to do more of, what you are doing well, and what to change – namely what you are doing badly. You then monitor the trend of your results over time.

Remember in Net Promoter it is more about the delta or direction of travel of your results than the actual number. That way you avoid issues of cultural bias, among others

Getting to the single reason why a customer gave a particular score will give some clear focus for the business to follow up; typically half a dozen themes will recur across a customer grouping if the question is posed at the same time as customers are being asked to give a score. This approach can apply equally to customers *and staff* – finding out what the staff issues are and how they link to customer issues is hugely revealing and work continues to confirm that employee advocacy driven through an inclusive approach has an impact on the end customer loyalty.

Customer or client effort

Back in July–August 2010, again in the *Harvard Business Review*, Matthew Dixon, Karen Freeman and Nicholas Toman introduced the Customer Effort Score (CES) as a metric. They focused on the need to move away from the obsession of trying to 'delight' customers that was turning into an epidemic of over-the-top service, to the detriment of both the company and the customer experience. They noted that customers defect from companies as a direct result of poor experiences and poor service. Their research addressed three key questions:

- How important is customer service to loyalty?
- Which customer service activities increase loyalty and which don't?
- Can companies increase loyalty without raising their customer service operating costs?

The two key findings were that delighting customers does not build loyalty and that reducing effort does build loyalty. You reduce effort by removing barriers that the customer faces – so, for example, if a bank account offers 10 benefits like airline lounges, mobile device insurance, travel insurance, etc. how easy do you make it to access those benefits? How much does the bank do versus putting the onus on the customer to activate these benefits? Or even simpler, do you force your customers to repeat their issue every time they are handed off during a call? Do you make customers call back repeatedly to resolve an issue?

The measure asks customers: 'How much effort did you have to put forth to handle your request?' Customers rate their experience on a scale of 1–5, where 5 represents very high effort and 1 very low effort required. Their research showed the positive predictive power of the Customer Effort Score in determining customer loyalty – which they defined as customers' intention to keep doing business with the company, increase the amount that they spend, or spread positive word of mouth. The CSI was the least predictive, NPS was good at the company level and CES outperformed both in service interactions.

This can be very powerful at an interaction level and can be used in conjunction with company-level NPS.

Customer expectation

Your Customer Effort Score can also be combined with a measure that I have used and which I consistently champion as a strong source of real customer feedback: the Customer Expectation Score – for which there is no acronym because Customer Effort Score has taken CES! The Customer Expectation Score is a three-point scale followed by a qualifying qualitative component. The question is:

Please select your answer from the following options. Did we:

a. 'Fail to meet your expectations?'

b. 'Meet your expectations?'

c. 'Exceed your expectations?'

Clearly it is asked after the event and is then supported by the simple statement,

'Please tell us why you gave that answer'.

What the customer expectation measure has is the advantage of asking the customer 'what they expected'. This is important because it does not assume that we already know what was important to that specific customer. If, as I contend, the true owner of a brand is the end customer and they have interpreted the advertising, previous experiences, friends, 'colleagues' comments to synthesise what they are actually going to expect, why try and second guess that? By asking what they expected, you are getting first-hand interpretations of the actual not assumed expectations.

You are also going to get highly actionable and specific data points to work with real time as the questions should be asked sufficiently close to the interaction for the customer to be able to recall without any difficulty.

For example, if the hotel survey just asked the Customer Expectation Score questions, guests are more likely to offer their views as it is short, simple and direct – it would leave it open for individual customers to provide feedback specific to them. Rather than hoping they will answer a 'is there anything else you would like to tell us?' question at the end of a one- to three-page questionnaire.

In a world where customer expectations are changing daily, particularly as technology advances, the idea of annual surveys should be redundant. As an example, some airlines now ask their customers to rate their flight before they have even got off the plane. The crew can get a rating before they have even disembarked at the destination, including what went well and what could be improved.

All of these have the benefit of potentially being real time and potentially predictive measures, giving an early indication of both positive and negative impacts on the customer, and link directly to customer feedback with internal analysis to provide a customer-validated priority list of remedial actions.

Indeed when used together I believe these three measures provide a very strong internal and external set of high-level measures linked to the ability to diagnose the root cause of both the positive and negative impacts.

Most importantly, having identified the issues you can put the tools and measures directly into the hands of those people in the organisation that can do something about them and impact on results

Converting existing measures into customer measures

The high-level customer measures that we have just reviewed provide a good dashboard for the leadership to review the customer experience. The challenge, however, is to make the customer measures relevant across the company.

You will find that individuals quite reasonably question their ability to influence such an all-encompassing company measure. In the same way that we have approached the challenge of changing the culture through a hundred and then eventually thousands of tiny changes the same can apply to measures. Your challenge is to find measures that already exist at local and personal levels and to badge those as the customer measures for that team or individual.

This is not as difficult as it might sound. For example, in finance you could badge invoicing errors as a customer measure as it directly impacts on the customer experience, creating customer complaints and generating costs through the required handling and corrective actions. Or consider in the case of an educational book supplier the key customer measures that the board needed to focus their attention on changed across the year. In the early part of their year the focus was on commissioning new books so the editors were centre stage; in the middle phase it was about getting the books produced and printed so the production team and their measures were the focus; in the final stage it was the finance, warehouse and logistics team who needed to get books out to schools on time and with accurate invoices. The key in this case was to have the board vary the measures that they concentrated on during the year, ending up with existing measures that were thought of as purely operational being rebadged a customer measure – in this case accurate picking, packing and delivery as schools cannot teach without their textbooks.

This approach has the advantage of not being seen to add to the already usually overly burdensome measurement frameworks that exist and being relevant to a variety of individuals in a variety of roles – often ones that would not normally be seen as impacting on the customer experience.

Remember you do not need to invent new measures – just use the ones you have and recognise that even operational-based measures can in fact be critical customer measures too

Retention measures are not a true guide to loyalty

The best practitioners of customer measures focus on acquisition, customer development and retention behaviour as an integral part of their customer measurement. Retention measures are extremely valuable for tracking past and current performance, but are unhelpful in predicting future performance or to identify areas of improvement.

For some industries, where there is little competition (due to product superiority, state provision of services, or simply high exit barriers), what are perceived as loyal customers may be either 'lazy' customers, or in some cases 'locked in' customers, often described as hostages, with few alternatives.

In B2B markets, apparently loyal customers can be trapped in high-priced contracts. Financial services suppliers have traditionally enjoyed high customer retention results, but these were mainly due to the high switching costs (hassle) involved, until new providers made it easy for their existing customers to switch (and when alternatives do become available there is switching on a massive scale).

Pursuing customer loyalty as a strategic imperative

In markets where the scope for growth through customer or competitor acquisition is limited, companies place greater strategic focus on retaining and developing their existing customer base. The loyalty of customers therefore becomes a strategic imperative.

Capturing the additional profit potential of customers through enhancing loyalty requires companies to go beyond customer satisfaction and create an experience that results in customers becoming advocates for the company and for its products, services or solutions.

The best companies do not leave loyalty to chance – they design it in so that it is integral to their culture, performance, outlook and brand.

Remember it is critical that this is not about the numbers, it is about what happens as a result of those numbers – findings must drive actions and then further measurement to see what is working

Things to think about

Customer experience is not about adding in a whole raft of new measures into your business.

Your approach for measuring your customer experience comes at two levels and should not necessarily involve increasing the burden of measures. You should consider the value of your current measures, including customer satisfaction and consider stopping them.

Your answer is to have a basket of *actionable measures* and to ensure that measures of the customer experience apply to all parts of the business. Look at rebadging an existing measure, consider how an individual's role contributes to the delivery of the overall customer experience, and ensure that the measure is relevant to the role and the individual and/or team.

When it comes to measures and reporting of measures, ask yourself the 'so what?' question. If you were to stop the measure tomorrow, what if anything would happen? One way to look at this is to ask who uses the measure, and what do they actually do as a result of the number or qualitative output being published.

As an example, consider the case of a new customer to a credit company. Effort is put into an experience in order to achieve an outcome – often this is for the company first and the customer second. The critical piece of data that determines the effort and investment that the company is willing to inject are the words 'we have a new customer'. Why, because now they cease to become a cost and start to pay down the acquisition cost.

This raises the question of when someone becomes a customer and also whether there is alignment in that measure across the company.

If you define the data point as when someone has an application approved you will create a very different outcome to a definition that says 'when the customer has used their credit card at least 10 times in a four-week period'. In effect by using that quantitative trigger you are extending the window of the acquisition experience to its natural conclusion. This causes problems because different teams are involved in putting the customer into the top of the funnel to those that are converting them to transacting customers.

Aligning what is essentially a piece of quantitative transactional data across internal silos makes it a potentially qualitative measure of the experience.

The greater the conversion from non-transacting to transacting customers, the likelihood is that a positive experience has been delivered. The driver of incentives and rewards and the point at which a customer is counted drives very different experiential activity.

If you are going to run an NPS or similar measure, keep it simple – look for the big messages and any trends over time, challenge the delivery team with the 'so what?' question. Ask them what they have in place in terms of no more than *three* actions resulting from the insights they have gleaned, ask what support they need from you, and then offer to provide whatever support they need to deliver.

9

How *small* data can make the difference

In the era of big data the experience world actually revolves around small data – we will see that single pieces of data can be critical to creating memorable experiences and challenge the theory that 'more is more' in terms of data in customer experiences. Does your data pass the 'so what?' test. Let's consider these questions:

- How do you find the important data?
- How can you use data to enhance experiences?
- How will legislation change the way we can use data?

For this chapter I decided to collaborate with an expert in the field of data but someone who also can act as the bridge between the twilight world of deep data and the real world of customer experience. When working with experts in data or technology my approach is always the same: I can describe what I need us to do for the customer, I can describe exactly how it needs to both look and feel for customers – I will leave you to figure out what needs to be done to deliver that behind the scenes. Frankly I don't want or need to know the details so long as the experience is delivered the way it has been designed. So meet Jonathan Carter, that unusual hybrid technical person who acts as my interpreter both ways – you will see his contribution later in the chapter.

Data can be a scary subject for an organisation to come to terms with: it is often seen as confusing, steeped in mystery and only truly understood by a few highly technical experts. Let's just consider some of the terminology used in the data world that creates this impression. Data scientist, analyst, decision scientist, data miner, 'big data', of course terabytes, and now that the internet traffic has grown so great it is measured in exabytes! Perhaps it should read 'terror bytes'? We are of course surrounded by data and our brains process huge amounts of data every single second, and it is this very scale that can make data seem to be too big to understand. Where do we even begin?

The customer area has probably been one of the greatest contributors to the big data storage warehouses that have developed over the past 20 years. The thirst for data driven by research departments, whether to analyse transactions or create loyalty schemes has meant that vast quantities of customer data remain stored almost in perpetuity, trillions of transactions are tracked every day and the investment in acquiring data is huge. Yet the returns are in many, many cases tiny or actually negative and in some cases never even tracked at all.

Ask yourself some basic questions:

- How much does your company spend on collecting data?
- . . . on storing data?
- . . . on analysing data?
- How do you create value from your customer data?
- How many people are employed in the company to collect, manage and analyse data?

Information or data is only valuable if it can be used to provide insights which then actually drive change. Sadly the most effort and expertise and applause is given to those who design and deliver incredibly complex statistical reviews of data over time – the beauty is in the complexity and the presentation not in the usability.

What is data? In my view it is very broad in terms of its definition: it can be a myriad of different things from a name and address, to a set of transaction histories, to a list of common issues endured by customers.

In my time as an executive my challenge at the end of a research or data debrief was always the same: 'so what?' I have spent £100k: what have I actually learned that is usable and I can connect to a return? Too often the reports simply confirmed what we already knew.

You need to understand broadly where the company is today in terms of its available customer data.

So following on from how much it costs:

- What do we do and how do we use data to improve customer experiences?
    - The first step is to do a basic rough audit. Find out what customer data do you capture – for example, what personal details do you capture? Do you capture transaction history, do you have a single view of your customer use of your products and services?
    - Understand what you are missing. For example, do you log calls and use the rich stream of information from customers that they contain? Do you log and categorise customer complaints and compliments?
- Who uses the data and how is data used?
    - Sort your data into quantitative and qualitative buckets (e.g. transactional, customer complaints/compliments, CSI, annual surveys, personal details, voice of customer programmes).
    - Is your data compliant in terms of privacy and permissions – i.e. can you use it?
    - Review the balance of customer data – quantitative versus qualitative – this reveals where the focus is in the business.
    - How accurate is the data? How many data errors occur – e.g. in a direct mail campaign how many email addresses come back as errors?

Remember a good start point is to examine what happens with a new customer or client – what data is captured, how is it stored, what permissions are sought and how is it used

This basic information is often hard to collate, which is an issue in itself, but will be useful as an indicator of the current health of your customer data. Additionally, this data will be useful both to challenge the data strategy in the future and to ensure you are able to draw on data to better design future experiences and to use data to identify and fix issues.

As the senior executive you should be asking the question: 'what is the return on investment of our data assets?'

Remember the ultimate question you are answering is not how much data do you have, but who has it and how is it used?

It can be helpful at this point to have some CJM software into which you can collate information – the structures that support these practitioner-developed tools will also act as a guide for you to approach your audit in a logical way. Why is this helpful? My preference is for the platforms that have been developed by practitioners because they will have done the initial thinking for you and know what type of information is likely to be out there to help you build out your customer journey data.

Having done this simple and basic audit you should stop looking for more data sources and instead wait until you are looking at a specific business issue from a customer experience design perspective. Too often data is looking for a home and a purpose, you need to review or create experiences and then look at the available data to support the delivery and identify any gaps.

Big data or small data?

So what is big data? According to Wikipedia:

'Big data is a term for data sets that are so large or complex that traditional data processing applications are inadequate. Challenges include analysis, capture, data curation, search, sharing, storage, transfer, visualization, querying, updating and information privacy. The term often refers simply to the use of predictive analytics or certain other advanced methods to extract value from data, and seldom to a particular size of data set. Accuracy in big data may lead to

more confident decision making, and better decisions can result in greater operational efficiency, cost reduction and reduced risk.'

As we noted at the start of this chapter, that is scary! What you should be thinking about is small data and how relevant pieces of information delivered or used at the right moment can be immensely powerful.

How often have you heard the expressions 'it's the little things that count', or perhaps 'the death of a thousand cuts'? Customer experience experts and professionals know that it is always the small personal touches that get noticed: the greeting by name, the smile, the 'please' and 'thank you', the gratis aperitif at the restaurant and the chocolate on the pillow or fresh flowers at the hotel.

These and countless other examples of the 'little things that matter' are what create the emotional connections covered earlier in Chapter 3, so aptly summed up by Maya Angelou in the quote highlighting the truism that 'people will never forget how you made them feel'.

It works in reverse of course: that annoying rattle in the car, the wrong name in communications, slow data connections/websites, long queues at the service desk, surly help on the shop floor, asking for the same information again and again – these will over time erode the customer experience and the customer's trust in brands that fail to see the value in getting the little things right!

Data from the customer interactions is the lifeblood for any organisation to view, understand and optimise the customer experience both remotely and on the front line! In the same way that customer experience experts understand that it's the little things that count, it's the *small* data that can make all the difference.

Of course big data can be used to power huge signposts or even predict customer experience issues and those road signs can then be used to drive corrective actions. Equally, if sufficient thought is put into the experience design then specific small pieces of data can be captured and used to deliver an enhanced customer experience. So data can be used both tactically and strategically – the common theme is that the requirement for that data has been determined by a customer experience. At one level you need to know if you are failing to deliver an expectation in sufficient time to recover the situation; at the other level you are actively collecting data to enable the delivery of a planned experience that is enabled by data.

Remember in both cases knowing about it is one thing, actively doing something about it is another

Consider the following as examples of each of these tactical and strategic influences on customer experience, each using data with a potential connection to experience.

A company issues contracts to clients on a regular basis; by their nature the contracts have a degree of complexity and the language used can be confusing and open to interpretation. The company regularly has client queries – read anxiety and stress for the client, meaning a degrading of their experience – about a particular clause. The company takes no action to mitigate this issue even though the data is available to show or predict that this will occur and it will inevitably have a negative impact on the client relationship. The cost of highlighting and explaining this clause in plain English perhaps using an example is minimal; the upside of saying 'can I just point out this [and maybe a couple of other specifics] clause and explain what this actually means as even I was confused when I read it' is significant in terms of trust.

At the strategic level consider the company behind the computer game *Destiny*. This game had an amazing $500 million investment plan before a game was ever sold. The game's producer Activision Blizzard said, 'of course we have very precise and well modelled projections of what we think the audience size is, who we think the game will or could appeal to if we market it correctly'. The game apparently has a multi-year rollout plan and data is at the heart of that plan and customer experience. How do I know this? Because my son is a *Destiny* player. Imagine how he felt when the latest release of the game was due and he was sent a link to a very high definition video clip. The clip used his name, spoke directly to him and used his real playing data. The level of engagement was amazing, his experience exceeded expectations. The company set out to collect very specific pieces of in-game data – they knew or predicted what the player would be interested in seeing but with a specific experiential outcome in mind. The data was collected over a period of months and then USED to great effect.

Remember in each of these examples it is not big data that is the answer, it is small, highly targeted pieces of data that can be used

It is not about deep data analysis to predict behaviour, it is about actively designing experiences and then applying data to enable the delivery. Cumulatively making lots of little changes using very specific pieces of data will aggregate to a bigger impact.

- Which of these examples demonstrates a company that uses data to improve the customer experience?
- What data do you collect on new customers?
- Do you design experiences and then apply data, or do data analysts prompt change in your company?
- Consider your business: what individual pieces of data do you need in order to improve or define your critical customer experiences?

The message is that the way to discover what you need is to design an experience from a customer perspective and then define what data you need to bring that to life.

What have we as customers experienced to date?

I remember a time when data about our customers and prospects was in short supply! Prior to the world of online communication – yes, there was one! – data about people, their names and addresses connected to that 'offline' ID, their attitudes, behaviours, preferences and intentions were subject to the laws of supply and demand and therefore relatively difficult and expensive to collect or buy, maintain and leverage in a privacy-compliant way!

This obviously became commoditised over time, but bad marketing practices and rogue customer data sources were common and the governance around that 'offline' customer data in terms of its accuracy, recency and levels of consent for marketing purposes was – shall we say – a little looser than it is today. This left room for some industries to become renowned for exploiting both those bad practices and rogue data, and in the process, contributing to a less than healthy reputation for direct marketing in the eyes of the consumer.

Remember that customers have a predisposition to mistrust companies that ask them for data based on a legacy of bad practices

Since that time, as we all know too well, the worlds of data technology and digital communications have collided and triggered the 'big bang' in terms of our data universe. That 'big data' universe is expanding at an ever-increasing rate as more of 'how' we as customers think and 'what' we actually do with our lives on a day-to-day basis – via mobile, apps, the internet of things, cars – becomes digitally connected.

Brands are strung out along a fairly long line in the process of moving down the path from direct marketing to data-driven marketing and customer experience with some barely off the starting line, but the reputational 'hangover' from the irresponsible use of data in earlier days of direct marketing still persists!

Consequently, as customer experience practitioners we have seen policy and legislation continue to tighten around data protection, privacy and data governance with the financial and reputational penalties and costs for breaking those rules becoming ever greater and customers becoming more aware of their rights under those rules.

Remember you should know the rules around data, so go online and check

For example, if you search for *European Regulation on Data Protection* you will find simple explanations of key shifts in policy. These regulations tend to have a ripple effect so you can expect similar changes in due course around the world.

The rise of this regulation does present you with an opportunity – this will be raising the data issue to the board level and it will begin to appear on risk registers: take advantage of that high profile.

It has now become and continues to grow as a significant source of organisational stress, marketing weakness and fundamentally a barrier to optimal customer experience for almost all organisations as they struggle to understand what they *can* and *can't* do in a legal and privacy-compliant way to leverage their customer knowledge, insight and awareness to engage the right customers and prospects, with the right message, at the right time, through the right channel and with the right tone of voice to deliver the best possible customer and prospect experience.

Remember, the answer is simple in principle – deliver a customer experience where the customer sees real value from how you use the data that they share with you and they will keep interacting/sharing that data and their consent for you to use it!

To balance my simple customer experience expert view of how you can use data, I asked Jonathan Carter to outline how that translates into a data and technology world – to give companies a chance to operationalise their data to help create the positive customer experiences that we design.

Using data to create a connected picture of your customers

A contribution by Jonathan Carter, Data Artist, an expert in creating legally and ethically compliant 'storyboards' for how data and marketing technology can be used to deliver sustainable trust, value and control to both the customer and the brand.

To get to the critical small data that lies at the heart of an optimised customer experience, there is no getting away from the need to move towards achieving a comprehensive and connected view of your customer data, ideally in real time and enterprise-wide across multiple channels and interactions that enables you to recognise and pick out the small but personal data variations between individual customers and their preferences.

To achieve this, you need to be able to identify and understand at an individual level how your customers are behaving across both traditional offline environments (if they exist in your business model) and, increasingly, the direct and indirect digital landscape where your customers are continuously exploring, interacting, communicating and self-publishing content.

As in the human central nervous system, some things people do are conscious and considered, while others are reflex actions, instinctive and sub-conscious. In the context of optimising the customer's journey, companies need to develop a range of trigger senses and response mechanisms that are similar in nature – reflex, instinctive and sub-conscious – a form of organisational muscle memory, helping your brand to listen, observe, adapt and respond to individual customer interactions either in or close to real time.

Remember, in order to react to the experiences of critical interactions during the customer journey you have to be able to sense and respond to customer interactions in the moment

Therefore, it is important that you view 'big data' from all customer and prospect interactions as a strategic resource rather than operationally as a business asset. You will start to see it not as something that your organisation owns in perpetuity, but more a 'natural' resource that needs to be nurtured, cared for and sustained by delivering individual product and service experiences to your customers that deliver genuine value exchange and as a result sustain both the business and data exchange from that customer.

The reality is that 'big data' is not the problem: 'big data' is just a resource and like any resource, the problem is rarely having too much of it! The problem is accessing it, connecting it to individual customers, refining and extracting the smaller parts that you need, when and where you recognise that you need them!

Remember you should be thinking if you have huge amounts of data on your customers, so what? How are you recognising where it fits and driving value for your customers and prospects from that data? This is where the 'small data' in the title of this chapter comes into play

Things to think about

Few companies are mature enough in customer experience terms to utilise the full value of the customer data at their disposal. Think small and start to use pieces of data to support the key customer interactions with your company.

You need to apply the same 'keep it simple, stupid' principle to begin to make progress, connecting data to customer experiences.

Start by looking through the other end of the telescope – so take a key interaction opportunity, design the experience and then reverse that into what data is needed to deliver your deliberate and purposefully designed customer experience. Recognise that there may be gaps in the data that is required; think about the examples earlier in this chapter.

Do not be taken in by the art of the possible.

Do review what you have today, what you spend and where the return is measured – you can even consider stopping where the return is not identified!

10

How to build trust through experience

As the world becomes more digital and companies seek to restrict personal contact, how will trust be built? As more and more data breaches hit the news, how can a company build trust in today's world?

- How does the experience that we have influence the level of trust that we feel?
- How many companies will we finally trust with our data and what competitive advantage will that give those companies?
- How is the data and privacy and regulatory environment the CE practitioner's friend today and into the future?

Using examples from financial services and telcos we will look at how experience can drive trust; we will also look at how we can really measure trust and how those that are in the vanguard are taking risks to create future advantage.

To discuss the role of trust in improving customer experiences, I've invited Martha Rogers, Ph.D. to contribute in a big way to this discussion. She and her business partner, Don Peppers, are considered to be two of the world's leading authorities on customer relationships built on trust. Their latest book is *Extreme Trust: Turning Proactive Honesty and Flawless Execution into Long-Term Profits* (2016). Dr Rogers has adapted some of their thinking, and the work done by her company, Trustability Metrix, for this chapter. How can experience drive trust?

How does experience impact on trust?

At its most basic level trust can be described as acceptance of the truth of a statement without the need for evidence – clearly this happens over time: initially evidence is required that you will do as you say you will and then, over time, you accept that this will happen without the need for evidence on each occasion. Hence the phrase 'we have learned to trust you'. Implicit in this statement is that there has been consistent evidence that you deliver your promise. For example, if you say you will not use my data beyond the stated purpose I believe you as you have proved that to be the case over time; or you promise to 'not make a drama out of a crisis', as one UK insurance company claimed in its advertising, when it comes to making a claim – and you actually deliver that experience.

The connection between what we expect to happen often based on advertising, written statements of service and similar versus the reality of what we actually experience is the basis for building trust. For this reason the customer experience is at the very heart of trusting a company or a brand.

Personal data and customer experience

As you look to design more personalised experiences, one of the key components that will enable you to do this is access to personal data on your customers. The ability not only to gather the relevant information but then also to have the permission to use that data will become increasingly difficult based on more prohibitive laws surrounding the privacy of the individual and rights to control data held by third parties. Without access to data and the correct permissions, companies are going to find the challenge of connecting to their customers will be significantly increased.

The more forward-thinking companies are today looking at what action is needed to turn what could be a legislative nightmare into an opportunity.

In the European market there are moves to significantly tighten and regulate in the whole area of privacy and permissions, most likely using the German model as the basis where some of the most stringent personal protections exist. In the future the idea of being opted into agreements to share your personal data will most likely be outlawed and even backdated, so if you don't have explicit permission to use a customer's data you will be banned from doing so. The active opt-in to data sharing will become the norm and those companies that we trust with our personal data will have a major competitive advantage.

The other area will be access to information that companies hold on us as individuals, where they will in future have to make all of that data readily and easily available to the individual.

From a customer experience perspective this is an ideal opportunity to get the customer into the risk register of the company and also to develop experiences that will inspire trust in the future. Leading-edge companies are already establishing tools for customers to self-manage their data through a dashboard. This is not dissimilar to the ability to manage location services on smartphones. The marketers see this as a real risk, trusting customers with the power to switch on and off with the potential to deny access to all of their data for anything other than the core service – this is described as the 'nuclear no' option. The reality is that if a customer chooses to exercise that option then the company has failed!

Ask yourself some basic questions:

- Could we respond to an information request from a customer to reveal all of the data held by our company on an individual?
- Is the data that we use for marketing and customer experience purposes auditable to ensure it has the required customer permissions for use?
- Do we operate a data opt-in or opt-out approach (in future it is very likely that you will only be able to use customer data where you have a verifiable opt-in from the customer)?
- Can customers change their data privacy preferences?
- Can customers self-manage the permissions they give us over time?

Regardless of your industry vertical, if you want to succeed you will need your customers to see you as reliable, dependable, credible, helpful, respectful, open, responsive and honest.

Dr Martha Rogers and colleagues have explored in-depth this issue of trust and customer experience. The following section explores in more detail some of the key findings from their studies and research conducted over the last few years.

The difference between mere trustworthiness and true trustability

By Martha Rogers, Ph.D., Founder, Trustability Metrix and Co-Founder Emerita, Peppers & Rogers Group, with Don Peppers, of Peppers & Rogers Group

What is 'TRUST', anyway?

Everybody's talking about 'trust' these days, and many use the term as a synonym for what we might call 'reputation', or 'regard', or 'popularity', or 'familiarity'. Brand equity like this is valuable and worth pursuing, but it's not the same as 'trustability', any more than fresh paint and a freshly mown lawn can reveal whether or not a house has a solid foundation.

For the most part, the business authors who've written about trust in the past have developed their own taxonomies to catalogue the various elements that make up trustworthiness, ranging from dependability and reliability to honesty and authenticity. These elements for 'trust' tend to boil down to a combination of *good intentions* and *competence*.

In other words, being *trustworthy* requires:

- doing the right thing; and
- doing things right.

Peter Drucker referred to doing things right as 'management'. (That's the competence, or 'execution' piece.) Doing the right thing? He called that 'leadership',[1] and that's the piece that's all about good faith, playing fair and best intentions.

The truth is, most real businesses don't abuse customers' and prospects' email addresses or mobile phone numbers or break

---

[1] Elizabeth Haas Edersheim and Peter F. Drucker, *The Definitive Drucker* (McGraw-Hill Professional, 2007), p. xi.

any laws. They don't violate their customers' trust like this for reasons that have little to do with the patchwork of regulatory restrictions enacted over the last two decades. In the transparent world we live in, this sort of behaviour would inevitably be exposed. So except for rapacious and disreputable fly-by-night marketers, companies refrain from doing these kinds of things at least partly because *they would be found out*. Even if there were no regulatory penalty at all, to be found abusing any person's contact details would immediately tarnish a company's reputation.

Most businesses today consider themselves to be trustworthy, and by yesterday's standards they are. They post their prices accurately, they try to maintain the quality and reliability of their products, and they generally do what they say they're going to do. But that's as far as most businesses go, and by tomorrow's standards it won't be nearly good enough. Not even close.

The fact is that far too many businesses still generate substantial profits by fooling customers, or by taking advantage of customer mistakes or lack of knowledge, or simply by not telling customers what they need to know to make an informed decision. They don't break any laws, and they don't do anything overtly dishonest. But think for a minute about the standard, generally accepted way some industries have made money for the past several decades:

- To credit card companies, a borrower who can never resist spending, rolls his balance from month to month, and often incurs late fees is considered a *most valuable customer*. The common industry term for a credit card user who dutifully pays his bill in full every month is 'deadbeat'.

- Mobile phone carriers profit from customers signing up for more expensive calling plans than their usage requires, and from roaming and data services accessed by accident.

A lot of traditional, widely accepted and perfectly legal business practices just can't be trusted by customers, and will soon become extinct, driven to dust by rising levels of transparency,

▶

increasing consumer demand for fair treatment,[2] and competitive pressure.

Customers are pretty particular about what they expect, and companies can be pretty slow at picking up on it. In one infamous study reported by Bill Price and David Jaffe, 80 per cent of executives thought their companies provided superior customer service, but only 8 per cent of the customers of those companies thought they received superior customer service.[3]

So if old-fashioned trustworthiness is not enough, what can we do instead that will make a real difference in a super-interconnected, completely transparent world? The answer lies in doing things right and doing the right thing, *and doing them proactively*. We've coined the term 'trustability' to encapsulate this new form of extreme trust, and what we mean by trustability is very simple: 'proactive trustworthiness'.

To be fully trustable, a company has to:

- do things right;
- do the right thing;
- be proactive.

So even though being *trustworthy* is certainly better than being untrustworthy, but soon even *trustworthiness* won't be sufficient. Instead, companies will have to be *trustable*. What's the difference?

Is your company careful to follow the rule of law? Do you train your people on your company's ethics policy in order to ensure compliance?

That's admirable, of course, and it's exactly what any trustworthy company must do.

But a *trustable* company would go further: rather than merely following the rule of law, a *trustable* company will follow the

---

[2] There have been many good-to-excellent books and articles written on trust. But one you should see is by our colleague Bruce Kasanoff, *No More Secrets: How Technology Is Making Honesty The Only Policy, digitaltrends.com*, 20 August 2012.

[3] Bill Price and David Jaffe, *The Best Service Is No Service* (Jossey-Bass, 2008).

golden rule towards customers and build its corporate culture around that principle.

Does your company try to do what's best for the customer whenever possible, balanced against your company's costs and financial requirements?

That's great, but a *trustable* company designs its business model purposely so as to ensure that whatever's best for the customer *is* financially better for the firm, overall.

A trustworthy company manages and coordinates all brand messaging to ensure a compelling and consistent story.

But a *trustable* company: recognises that what customers and other people say about the brand is far more important than anything the company says about itself.

A trustworthy company focuses on quarterly profits as the most important, comprehensive, and measurable KPI.[4]

But a *trustable* company: uses customer analytics to balance its quarterly profits against changes in its customers' long-term value.

Rather than simply working to maintain honest prices and reasonable service, in the near future companies will have to go out of their way to protect each customer's interest *proactively,* taking extra steps when necessary to ensure that a customer doesn't make a mistake, or overlook some benefit or service, or fail to do or not do something that would have been better for the customer.

How businesses will practice proactivity

What would it really mean for a business to be *proactively trustworthy,* rather than merely 'trustworthy'? Let's just explore what trustability would mean for a mobile telephone carrier. The typical mobile carrier today is not very proactive about protecting the interests of its customers. Within an environment of smartphones and increasingly capable wireless services, the charges a mobile carrier assesses can be complex, and complexity presents a

---

[4] Key Performance Indicator.

▶

tempting opportunity to take advantage of customers. It might involve allowing customers to incur unintended data charges, or it might be failing to put a customer on the most beneficial or cost-efficient calling plan for their usage patterns. Or it could result from simple neglect (categorised as incompetence): if a customer is due to get a new phone at the end of his two-year contract, for instance, but doesn't notice when a period of two years elapses, a trustable mobile phone company would proactively remind him and invite him to come in to choose a new one. However, most mobile operators do not, preferring to 'let sleeping dogs lie', and continue to collect on a fully paid-up contract while waiting for the customer to request an upgrade for some other reason.

Since genuine trustability requires being completely transparent, if a customer is about to subscribe from a home or business address prone to poor network coverage or slow broadband con-nectivity, a trustable telecom company would advise him or her in advance of this weakness in its offering, perhaps providing a discount or other benefit until such time as service in the cus-tomer's home area is improved. The best strategy for a mobile carrier with a weakness in its offering is simply to communicate frankly about flaws and weaknesses in advance, as a way to inspire customers that they can have confidence in the compa-ny's suggestions and recommendations.

So what's the key question? *How much more would a customer be willing to pay to do business with a mobile carrier he consid-ers to be trustable?*

Why your CFO will learn to love trustability

Our company, Peppers & Rogers Group, fielded a research survey to develop some top-line insights with respect to how customer trust affects certain kinds of businesses.[5] We began by asking respondents how much they thought their mobile services pro-vider could be trusted, based on the kinds of behaviours listed here.

---

[5] Thanks to Tom Lacki for his additional insights about the research on trust-ability and mobile carriers.

Trusters were much more likely than distrusters to say that they would buy more things from their carriers without hesitation, including new data services, additional lines and upgraded phones. Trusters also said they would be more likely to remain as customers for a longer period, citing a strong sense of emotional loyalty to their mobile carriers. In addition, far more trusters than distrusters said they felt no need to search for alternatives and would recommend their carrier to others and defend it from criticism.

The most significant additional finding from the research was that participants said *they would be willing to pay about US$11 more per month*, on average, for a mobile carrier consistently demonstrating a higher level of trustability. More than one of the American mobile carriers can boast about 70 million customers. So let's do the maths: if you run a telecom company and your customers would be willing to pay you an extra $11.00 per month, times 12 months a year, that is about US$1.3 billion for every ten million customers per year in incremental revenue, or nearly $9 billion for one of those big carriers. Only a fraction of this would be needed to accomplish most of the trustable actions described earlier. The rest would drop to the company's bottom line, increasing customer satisfaction in the short term and loyalty in the long term.[6]

The overall conclusion of our extensive research is that although the financial benefits of earning the trust of customers may or may not show up in current-period results, there can be little doubt that trustworthiness and its higher standard, trustability, have the potential to return significant benefits over the long term.

Why are so many companies having a hard time moving from mere 'trustworthiness' to truly competitive 'trustability'?

Companies cannot simply ignore the reputational damage if they resort to untrustworthy activities and customer experiences that don't match their customer expectations. But unfortunately, while

---

[6] Our understanding of the difficulties of operating a mobile carrier in a more trustable way came from an interview we did with Peppers & Rogers Group consultants responsible for this client, Ozan Bayulgen and Zeynep Manco, Peppers & Rogers Group Istanbul office, August 2011.

economics may not be everything, when it comes to operating a profit-making company with a payroll to meet and shareholders to satisfy, it's *almost* everything. It's extremely important to realise, therefore, that while acting in a customer's interest may often require a company to incur a short-term cost, it will nearly always be economically beneficial for your company in the long run, and sometimes dramatically beneficial.

Ironically, at the heart of most companies' untrustable behaviour is a nearly manic obsession with short-term financial results and almost total disregard for longer-term financial implications. Short-termism generates many dysfunctional and even self-destructive business practices, as profit-oriented companies dismiss the long-term consequences of their actions in order to generate current-period profits – profits that feed the bonus pool, pump the stock price and meet analysts' expectations. Short-termism is usually connected to unadulterated self-interest and directly conflicts with trustability, but it is still easily the most pervasive and destructive business problem on the planet today.

The truth is, however, that short-termism only reigns supreme at most businesses because *the financial metrics we apply to business are not economically true measures of success*. They never have been, and they haven't substantially changed since being introduced at the beginning of the industrial age. The way most businesses 'do the numbers' to document their financial performance focuses entirely on the past – that is, on the most recent financial period. Most companies' financial reports to shareholders include absolutely no consideration of the way the most recent performance has or has not delivered on their customer experiences or promises, or delivered their customers' expectations and therefore either helped or harmed your company prospects for generating future profits, leaving this detail to the stock market analysts and others to figure out.

Managers sometimes take comfort in the sophistication and precision of their short-term financial metrics, ignoring the long-term effects simply because they can't be as precisely defined. But remember the simple fact about business metrics: if you aren't measuring the right things to begin with, you're not going to get better results by measuring them more accurately.

Customer experience and relationships: a link to long-term value

When it comes to understanding how trustability creates financial value for a business, there are basically two approaches to the issue: a simple, philosophical approach and a quantitative, analytical approach. Both start with customers, for one simple reason: by definition, all the revenue you will ever generate will come from the customers you have now and the ones you will have in the future. (Take note: brands, products, patents, logos, sales regions and marketing campaigns do not pay money to a firm; only customers do.) The simple approach is to state your company's value proposition as a straightforward quid pro quo:

1. You want each customer to create the most possible value for your business.

2. On the whole, a customer is likely to create the most value *for* you at about the point he gets the most value *from* you.

3. The customer gets the most value from you when he can *trust* you to act in his own interest.

To maximise the value your customers create for your business, you need to earn and keep their trust – that is, to act in their interest and to be seen doing so.

It is your relationship with an individual customer, and the resulting experience you create for him, in other words, that provides the 'missing link' between your company's short-term, current-period earnings and its long-term, ongoing value as a business enterprise. Apply this philosophy to enough customers and you'll be able to overcome the temptation of short-termism.[7]

---

[7] Serious readers are encouraged to turn to *Return on Customer: Creating Maximum Value from Your Scarcest Resource* (Currency/Doubleday, 2005), by Don Peppers and Martha Rogers, Ph.D., for a comprehensive discussion of the statistical, mathematical and practical issues involving calculation of up-or-down changes in individual customer lifetime values. As an operating business creating value for shareholders, customer equity is virtually the same as a company's economic value, because the economic value of any business is the discounted net present value of all future cash flow yet to be generated by the business. Also see Don Peppers and Martha Rogers, Ph.D., *Rules to Break and Laws to Follow: How Your Business Can Beat the Crisis of Short-Termism*, 2008.

▶

How trustable companies use customer insight to improve customer experience

Even though no company can ever be certain what's in any particular customer's mind, companies today do have much more capable technologies for analysing their customers' needs and protecting their interests by providing positive customer experiences. Sometimes, all that's required is for a company to use its own processes to help a customer avoid a costly and preventable mistake. Peapod, the online grocery service, for instance, has software that will check with you about a likely typo before you buy something highly unusual ('Do you really want to buy 120 lemons?').[8]

The best companies are also using their greatly improved IT capabilities to do a better job of remembering their customers' individual needs and preferences. A trustable company will remember what it learns about each customer, becoming smarter and more insightful over time, and then using this insight to create a better customer experience. Sometimes, all that's required is for a company to use its own database of past customer transactions for the customer's benefit.

If you order a book from Amazon or a song from iTunes that you already bought from the company, you will be reminded before your order is processed.

These are examples of genuinely trustable behaviour. In each case, the company's database gives it a memory that can sometimes be superior to the customer's memory. It would not be cheating for Amazon or iTunes simply to accept your money, thank you very much. Rather than using their superior, computer-powered memory to *take advantage* of the customer, however, Amazon and iTunes use it to *do the right thing*.

Note that 'the right thing' to do, at least in this case, is mutually beneficial. Even as Amazon offers you the chance to opt out of a purchase you've already made, they also reduce the likelihood that you'll receive the book, realise you already have it, and return

[8] The Peapod example comes from Ian Ayres, *Super Crunchers: Why Thinking-by-Numbers Is the New Way to Be Smart* (Bantam, 2007), p. 170.

it. When iTunes warns you you're about to duplicate a song you already own, they are making it less likely they'll have to execute a labour-intensive and costly refund process, or that you'll think badly of them aloud on Twitter. This is exactly how 'reciprocity' is supposed to work – as a win–win.

Ironic isn't it? That some banks use their customer databases and analytics tools to craft highly sophisticated pictures of their customers' and prospects' value, profitability and credit risk and then bombard them with two billion credit card solicitations every year. Why don't more of them do what Royal Bank of Canada (RBC) has done? RBC has used its superior insight to extend automatic overdraft protection (with no fee!) to low-risk customers (that is, *most* customers). That way, the customer gets a break – and so does the bank: instead of having to pay a service rep to handle a call from a reliable customer who demands the fee be rescinded, the bank chooses instead to send a note explaining 'this one's on us' and how to avoid this in the future, reducing their own costs in the process. Rather than incurring costs and resentment, and then netting no fee anyway, the bank saves the costs, builds goodwill and *then* nets no fee. During the first 10 years after instituting this approach, RBC increased per-customer profitability by 13 per cent.[9]

In conclusion: ask yourself these simple questions

How many of your customers could agree enthusiastically with the following statements:

- I can depend on this company to do the right thing for me.
- I know this company will make sure I get the right deal.
- This company does things right and makes it easy for me.
- I have a great experience when I do business with this company.
- I would be willing to tell people I know how much I trust this company.

---

[9] We did the research on Royal Bank of Canada for our textbook revision, Don Peppers and Martha Rogers, Ph.D., *Managing Customer Experience and Relationships: A Strategic Framework*, 3rd edn. (Wiley, 2016).

▶

- I would be willing to pay a little more to do business with this company.
- I trust this company more than I trust their competition.

As standards for trustability continue to rise, the companies, brands and organisations shown to lack trustability will be punished more and more severely. Very soon, for competitive reasons, all businesses, old and new, will begin to respond to the increase in demand for trustability by taking actions that are more worthy of trust from the beginning – that is, actions that create better customer experiences – actions that are more transparently honest, less self-interested, more competently executed, less controlling and more responsive to others' inputs: more proactively trustworthy. Trustable.

(Adapted from Don Peppers and Martha Rogers, Ph.D., *Extreme Trust: Turning Proactive Honesty and Flawless Execution into Long-Term Profits,* ©2015, 2016. Used in this edition of this book with special permission of the author.)

Things to think about

Dr Rogers has made the case that the leading companies in terms of customer experience recognise that *it is in a company's own economic self-interest to be trustworthy,* and in future those that do not choose to accept this will be forced to consider the implications of being seen as untrustworthy.

- How many companies would you trust in the future with your personal data and what would you allow them to do with that data?
- Would you trust your company to have access to and to use your personal data?

Remember the active opt-in to data sharing will become the norm and those companies that we trust

with our personal data will have a major competitive advantage

- Consider for a moment who you would consider trustworthy enough to use your data and perhaps who could be considered as a gatekeeper for your data in the future.

- Would you trust your own company – what is the experience that you offer today that will inspire trust from your customers to the extent that they are prepared to give you access and permission to use your personal data?

- This issue is now being talked about in terms of good profits and bad profits, where the latter are driven out of cheating customers, charging exorbitant fees and generally damaging customer experiences. For example, how can a bank justify the fees charged for sending out letters; how can airlines justify the huge fees for an administrative change to a ticket; how can entertainment ticketing companies justify their booking fees?

- Consider your company. Does it have any practices that are clearly generating bad profits?

Measuring trust is an area that is still 'under development' but the business outcomes of trust are clear to see in terms of your stock performance through to your average spend per customer. One route for those looking to be in the vanguard of the trust agenda is provided by the team at Trustability Metrix where they are developing a more and more sophisticated tool to measure high-level trustability based on customer perception, employee perception, KPIs and business practices, and reviews both what the company says it will do and the internal capability to deliver on that promise.

Trustability matters throughout our efforts to build better customer relationships and experiences but there is an immediate issue that demands attention.

The leading companies in terms of customer experience recognise that *it is in a company's own economic self-interest to be trustworthy* – in future those that do not choose to accept this will be forced to consider the implications of being seen as untrustworthy.

11

How to equip and support teams for success

It happens all too often that those charged with responsibility for the delivery of customer experience programmes are inadequately equipped to carry out the task. This chapter looks at the root cause of failure and the way to reverse this by creating conditions to thrive for both the people and the strategies. Think about these questions:

- Why do customer-based transformations nearly always fail?
- Where does the customer sit on an organisation chart?
- Do we need a chief customer officer?

Few, if any, senior executive training courses focus on equipping leaders to manage the customer component of their balanced score-card. The resulting lack of confidence at a leadership level creates problems at an executional level in the company. We will look at how leaders can absorb the customer component and effectively lead their teams without even breaking step with the rest of their work. The issue of this being new and additional in an already full diary will be explored and examples of how the customer can be integrated into everyday activities illustrated.

Increasingly the customer experience is featuring in job adverts so what can be done to set up a chief customer officer (CCO) or customer experience lead for success and avoid the early pitfalls of integrating this new customer management discipline into your organisational design?

In the last 20 years we have seen the importance of the customer rise in the consciousness of the business world, even if at times it might have happened unconsciously! So, more and more senior executives quote the customer experiences as one of their top three strategic drivers for the next financial year. The problem is that this has been the case for the last 10 years but nothing has actually changed. Back in 2003 Lippincott Mercer research described customer experience as the next 'business tsunami'; well 13 years on we are still waiting! Yes there have been a few small waves but if we ask the question 'how many successful customer experience-based transformations can you name?' the answer is close to if not zero. This begs the question, 'why?' Against a backdrop of strong strategic imperatives, why have businesses singularly seemed to have failed to deliver long-term change? Twenty years ago there was little by way of an expert support base or network available and few tools to support the internal external customer agenda. Today there are specialist businesses that have grown in what was initially a niche area: customer journey mapping is regularly deployed as an outside-in customer view, measurement frameworks have evolved such as we have covered earlier and they are supported by a growing software capability (like SuiteCX). Yet the almost-weekly launches of laudable programmes targeting improvements to the way businesses look after their customers remain doomed to failure.

It could be claimed that the global financial crisis brought the customer question into the boardroom in a way never previously experienced. As global corporations previously thought impregnable failed day after day, the survivors launched an unprecedented wave of slash and burn to try and rescue balance sheets and profit & loss statements (P&Ls) – who can forget the scenes of office workers leaving buildings carrying cardboard boxes containing the remnants of a career? The maturity of social media has further added to the backlash. Of course this was no more than a temporary stitch in place – the smarter businesses began to realise that cutting costs is a blunt instrument and if you don't know where to cut in the first place it can leave you with lower costs but haemorrhaging customers, sales and of course profits. The deteriorating customer experience added further weight to an increasingly negative customer sentiment towards some brands that converted into 'customer flight' and a vicious downward spiral.

Every cloud has a silver lining and this was to some extent the case for the nascent customer experience discipline: the need to retain customers was now an urgent boardroom matter that embattled

CEOs needed to take control of. If it wasn't there before, the mission and vision now clearly stated that customers are important, usually expressed in colourful language like 'passionate', 'love' or 'customers first'!

One of the biggest causes of failure for customer experience activity is of course that the words are very easy to say and many thousands of CEOs will have stood up at conferences and told the assembled leaders that the customer is their driver or something similar – indeed the customer agenda is perfect for corporate sound bites for use internally, with investors and the media. To understand why these statements can be made by the most senior figures and yet continue to fail to deliver we need to consider the DNA of customer experience transformation programmes (CETPs) – how do they start, how do they grow and how do they fail?

What usually follows a conference announcement is the initiating of a company-wide transformational programme – let's call it 'customer first' with the accompanying 'we are in it together' sign off. The Herculean task of transforming the company to one driven by its customers is then 'gifted' to an executive who in most cases handles this 'honour' in the same way that you might handle an angry king cobra by then passing this honour down the line to a programme team. So we have already passed the true accountability down to a level where the individual or team are very constricted in terms of their ability to make changes and those who should be accountable will be in review and critique mode next time the subject comes across their desks.

Your deployment then follows a familiar and depressing format:

- establish a major programme complete with massive and stifling governance and reporting;
- continue to transfer responsibility downwards;
- create a two-year timeline where the deliverables will solve 'world peace';
- review the current state, typically focusing on IT, processes, and infrastructure, not because they are the key components but because that is where businesses are most comfortable;
- create business cases;

- try to get onto your executive-crowded agendas in order to justify the need for change to the very people who initiated it;

- kill other positive ideas for change on the grounds that the programme has or will have this covered and all will be delivered in two years' time;

- deal with executive sponsors that have more important things to do than work on your customer agenda and instead turn up for a 30-minute opening address at important meetings and perhaps to have findings reported back to them (of course what this subliminally tells the team is that there are more important things to do than their work);

- 'enjoy' and endure the constant chipping away by unconvinced colleagues who as they don't have line responsibility feel free to undermine the agenda and feel threatened by change they don't understand ('we are already running a profitable business, tell me why we need to change?');

- watch your original sponsor be promoted or leave and see the customer agenda reduced to the 'angry teenager in the basement' again – and worst of all watch the CEO leave and wait for the notification to stop as the new CEO conducts a 'strategic review'.

This may seem an unnecessarily dark picture, but it is the reality for many customer-based programmes around the world today. The impact is to set back the customer agenda by years inside the business as it is seen as a failure and other options are then given priority – in many ways it would have been better never to start on such a journey.

These problems begin as soon as the proverbial genie is out of the bottle, which is when the CEO stands up in public and says we are going to focus on our customers – of course what he or she means is you are going to try and focus on your customers until something more short term and important comes along.

No one will ever argue with the sentiment or even the business logic, but nothing in an individual's career to date has prepared them to answer the question 'how will I/should I contribute to a customer agenda?' – in many cases they then take the view that on analysis this 'customer piece' does not affect me so I will carry on as normal until I have to engage in my role as chief financial officer, sales director, legal counsel, IT director, operations director, logistics director; the list goes on. This could not be further from the truth: customers impact on everyone and everyone impacts the customer. In the world of business, the customer is unique in that it has the capability to bust silos – it is hard to argue with what your customer says about your business and its failings, hence the challenge and the threat it poses.

Here are just a few examples of what you can do to educate the wider team, reduce the fear factor and instil confidence that improvements are deliverable:

- Provide senior leaders with support through coaching, mentoring, awareness sessions that will equip them to actively engage with the customer experience with confidence.
- Review the current training and development courses that you run or buy in. See where you can inject customer experience into these existing programmes.
- Introduce a customer experience module into your senior executive training programmes – look to inject the customer into other components of these established programmes.
- Engage in CJM work.
- Provide opportunities to introduce the customer voice into the business at different levels.

This becomes a matter not of strategy but of culture, behaviours and capability and we all know that 'culture eats strategy for breakfast'. The often prevailing but unspoken view that 'I'm not going to sacrifice my career over this' is revealed through a passive-aggressive response from those in positions of power and influence that transmits deep into their teams and gives the tacit green light to a range of negative and blocking behaviours. In effect the body rejects the new 'organ' and slowly but surely defuses it, usually through a slow but inevitable death by a thousand cuts. Interestingly, when I operated in China this was not allowed to happen as a direct consequence of CEO-level leadership and intervention throughout the activity. Not only does this cultural smothering mean that the original-perceived benefits would never crystallise, but also, as mentioned earlier, the customer agenda is damaged for the future and huge amounts of emotional energy have been wasted in the attempt.

We are all, to a greater or lesser extent, scared of the unknown and the management of the customer component of a strategy sits firmly in the unknown or limited knowledge box. Individuals almost always look after number one and take short-term views, responding to the last order given – so should we really be surprised that CETPs are doomed to failure?

If we look at the average tenure of a CEO as three years and then follow the formula: year one, stop everything and have a strategic review; year two, make some changes and hope market conditions favour you on the stock price; year three, what is my legacy project?; year four, 'reset to year one' for the new CEO. It is against this backdrop that a customer revolution is attempted – not exactly conditions to thrive from the top.

If we accept that this scenario is playing out around the world – and my personal evidence is conclusive that it is – then consider that one definition of madness is 'doing the same thing and expecting the outcome to be different' and we have to ask the question, 'can businesses improve their chances of success in the customer component of their strategy?'

Can we find a different approach that might have an improved chance of success in engaging businesses with their colleagues and customers for mutual benefit? Twenty years of experience of watching this happen and experimenting with different approaches suggests 'yes we can'.

Remember that at the heart of the issue is that business leaders, often unintentionally, miscommunicate the goal – the challenge is how to articulate and describe what you are setting out to achieve and then to manage our human reaction to it

At the outset, language is critical – so, for example, what does 'transformation' mean? According to the businessdictionary.com it is 'a process of profound and radical change that orients a business in a new direction and takes it to an entirely different level of effectiveness' – that is enough to scare away even the most seasoned of executives.

As we have seen, the subconscious reaction to this is negativity driven by fear and lack of understanding. What does the sound bite 'we are going to be passionate about our customers' break down into in terms of concrete actions and therefore practical relevance to an accounts clerk? In the absence of immediate relevance, individuals wait to be told what to do and the changes rarely seep down to that level before the programme is pulled or replaced with another business priority. This question of relevance is significant in the early stages of any customer activity – the sooner that individuals can see how they can or are going to be required to contribute through their day-to-day actions will impact on the ability to evolve the culture. It must be noted that teams usually receive initiatives that seek to improve the customer experience very well, but they simply don't believe that the will is there to actually follow through and deliver. Imagine if the same CEO not only produced the sound bite, but also backed that up with some concrete examples of how they personally would be contributing to the customer component of the business strategy.

Remember that for change to happen it has to be relevant at a local and individual level

All managers and most of the staff in a company that has been established for many years recognise that even if the words are said, the reality is that the company will not place the customer as the overarching arbiter of decisions and strategy in the company. Sitting in the audience there is therefore a heavy dose of well-founded cynicism about what will actually happen. The myriad of metrics, targets, programmes and strategies in business as usual precludes such a change.

Remember what is actually needed is to elevate the customer to a position

of at least parity with the other strategic and cultural influencers – pricing, product, infrastructure, etc

The objective is to equip the business and its people to use the customer view as another lens or prism through which to consider strategy, review business decisions and engage with colleagues.

As we have noted, when a major IT investment comes before the company investment appraisal group, the customer question is what is the impact on me during the install and during ramp up? – this needs to be understood and it may be mitigating actions need to be costed and put in place.

A similar view can be taken on the impact on colleagues and what is required to equip those colleagues in the front line to handle customer issues that may arise and could cause significant brand equity damage.

At the other end of the spectrum should I answer the ringing phone that may be a customer, or should I ignore it and finish the time-sensitive report that my boss wants on her desk by 2 p.m.? The former may only occur a handful of times a year, but the latter can occur hundreds of times a day around the world.

The solution is not to create a programme and effectively ring-fence ownership and accountability – you can almost feel the palpable sense of relief once a colleague has the ball and others can get back to their day jobs. This also allows the sniping from the sideline to begin as collective responsibility is abandoned. In effect, the programme becomes a target to be shot at and inevitably the programme focus tends to be on the easy bit to work on – the process – rather than the hard bit of evolving the culture (how many programme objectives have cultural change as a critical objective?).

Drawing the customer into the culture of the business impacts on all, and *all* have to be engaged.

With programmes come governance: ask yourself the question, 'is that governance there to protect the customer or is it there to protect the company's interests?'

The solution is not to announce major customer programmes but rather to set a hundred small challenges, then a hundred more, and engage people at local levels with small-scale, easy to execute changes without the labels of transformational change. If colleagues don't feel threatened then the defences will not be raised, and once small changes begin and confidence grows the momentum will be self-generating.

From a senior leadership perspective there needs to be subtle evidence of behavioural changes: questions being asked and targets being either adjusted or given different levels of focus.

For example, imagine as the CFO asking the question, 'when was the last time we reviewed the wording on our standard letters to make sure they are customer friendly and in line with our brand?'

Or as the CIO, 'what were the impacts on the customer experience of our recent systems outage and what plans do we have to mitigate that in future?'

To achieve this the company needs to engage in equipping its entire people to 'think differently': to consider a customer lens when reviewing both issues and opportunities. Senior executives need to know how and when to challenge and question colleagues to drive and underpin the behaviours needed to engage with the customer agenda. Managers and frontline staff need to be equipped with the, often new, tool of a customer view to manage both the day to day and the evolution of the business over time. The business can then grow muscle to evolve and embrace the customer as a part of its decision-making processes.

The mantra is a hundred tiny changes ... then a hundred more ... and then a thousand, and so on – delivered by a wide range of individuals throughout the business. With this approach comes the perhaps shocking but very pleasant revelation that these hundreds of changes which together, over time, amount to real change often cost nothing and may even reduce cost – impacting positively on both sides of the balance sheet.

A board or a customer experience team cannot change a business on their own; they can create the platform from which change can happen, but for the culture to evolve you will require the active engagement of the majority of your staff – whether they realise that they are involved or not. Just consider a team of 10 tasked with managing customer-based changes and how much they can achieve when compared to having 5,000 colleagues each doing one thing differently. The critical people to have engaged are your middle management layer that both engage upwards and have real day-to-day control of most of the functions of your company.

You must avoid being seen as a burden: someone layering on another task onto already stretched and busy people. If you can incorporate a customer focus into my daily routine then that is manageable – it must also be relevant to me, my role and potentially be measurable too.

From an organisational design perspective there remains an issue of how to integrate an emerging management discipline into the existing organisational structure. Currently there remains uncertainty around where it best fits: is it a commercial role; does it sit within brand or marketing; is it a standalone business function? Where should this report in line terms – direct to the CEO, the COO, or perhaps the sales and marketing team? My view is that this should be a partnership with the CEO with the authority to influence across business functions.

In time we will see the discipline as a function in the same way as sales or marketing, but it does have a business-wide influence, given that the experience impacts everyone and everyone impacts on the experience. What has emerged is a trend towards the deployment of chief customer officers and senior customer experience leads – this has been explored in great and practical detail by Jeanne Bliss in her leading work on this subject, *Chief Customer Officer 2.0* – a book well worth reading!

The problems facing chief customer officers or customer experience leads

Has the appointment of the chief customer officer, or perhaps the senior vice president customer experience, taken over from the setting up of a customer service initiative as the quick fix to becoming more customer focused, and thereby neatly addressed the whole issue of how the company and in particular senior executives need to engage? What better than to put it all into the basket of a named individual and let them get on with the accountability and responsibility, but usually without the authority! It certainly sends a signal to the organisation and potentially to customers that you are serious about the importance of your customers, but if the appointment and the implications are not thought through the result is, in the medium and possibly short term, that little more than a thin veil is drawn over the area and both staff and customers very quickly see through it – this is like putting a sticking plaster on a huge wound. Deployed well, the appointment can be the catalyst to real action and the nucleus around which true customer focus can aggregate.

The key problem facing these new appointees is that they are often in a team of one and vested with little or no executive authority, and they have to work what magic they can through force of personality and influence. It is also key to note that the role should go through some transitions, typically from front running, 'tub thumping' motivator with much attention centred around the individual but moving to a position where the energy, enthusiasm and day-to-day activities are taken up by a growing variety of individuals inside the business at all levels and in all areas, making the customer agenda business as usual and then the lead becomes more of the conscience of the business and the facilitator who 'greases the wheels' to make things happen. This does not happen by accident and requires a plan and a clear approach from the individual charged with the task, and clearly articulated support of different types, over time, to assure the execution and the business benefit.

To add to the difficulties posed by the roles being relatively new, the appointees are often asked to write their own job descriptions and to provide proposed scope, or at the least to define what their business objectives might be. Uncertainty tends to exist at all levels of the business about what this new lead role is responsible for delivering – colleagues are happy to be supportive as long as the new role does not impact on or try to unduly influence their plans in their clearly defined areas of responsibility. If this situation arises, and it is almost inevitable that it will, disputes will result and the default decision on what takes precedence is a reference to financial objectives, and unless the customer experience lead has direct P&L impact the chances are that they will be the loser or the one to compromise. In a worst-case scenario, in a large corporate it is easy to stifle one individual by 'ganging up' or insisting on a whole series of approvals – in political circles this would be classified as 'filibustering'. So making the link between experience and the bottom line is business critical early in any tenure in such a post.

From the other end of the telescope the new lead often has to try to balance out two agendas internally: a need to exert some central authority and demonstrate added value, while gaining the trust and support and often budget from the operating units. The result is slow progress and no one party particularly satisfied. This situation is not helped by the way in which customer experience lead roles tend to be both born and then sourced – either a high-level recognition that customer experience is important and that the way to recognise this is to create an executive post, which often leads to an external appointment as no one on the current team knows what they would do; or the alternative route is that a highly motivated individual who has had commercial success executing a customer experience programme in a localised area, region or business unit, often driven by their own passion but always having some authority to deliver, is elevated to a centre-based role and asked to replicate their success on a wider scale across the business. In the case of the former there is often a credibility gap and a lack of knowledge about 'how to get things done'; and in the latter there is often resistance from colleagues back in operating units to the newly elevated individual rather than what they can achieve.

The challenge then is to think about the logic that leads to the view that there is a need for a customer experience lead and then to consider how that may be executed to maximise the probability of success for both the individual and the company. A simple approach to this is to step through the key stages of analysis of a business problem – why, what and how?

Why appoint a customer experience lead?

There are a number of possible reasons why thoughts turn to the area of customer experience and in particular to the executional option of appointing a lead for the business. As we noted earlier these can often be necessarily based on business negatives – for example:

- because more and more companies now realise that the customer experience is the next competitive battle ground;
- because if you don't give your customers a better experience someone else will;
- because you need someone to represent customers, in the boardroom and across the whole organisation;
- because you need to understand customers' wants and needs and to make sure that you deliver against them;
- because you need to understand customer value and how to allocate resources to increase that value; and overall
- because you need someone to bring this all together and be an agent for change.

What are the benefits of having a customer experience lead?

- it will improve business results, by focusing on what will increase revenue and reduce costs;
- it makes the customer experience visible and gets the whole organisation behind it;
- it raises the customer experience to a strategic rather than tactical level;
- customer issues get more attention and people understand their role and the contribution they can make;
- it makes it easier to identify and allocate the right resources;
- it will help to prioritise activities and to make the business case for new initiatives, and to identify and exploit the quick wins;
- it will help to increase customer loyalty and advocacy, leading to increased customer value and increasing returns; and finally
- this will be the catalyst and person who leads the transformation towards a more customer-focused organisation.

What sort of person do I need?

- You need someone who has the confidence of the senior team, especially the chairman or CEO. It is likely that they will already be performing a key role in the business or have a significant customer experience management discipline in either a consulting or line management capacity in a similar role in another company.
- You need someone with a passion for customers and customer service – and who can instil this passion in others.
- You need someone with a broad functional knowledge, for example in:
  - managing people;
  - operations;
  - project and programme management;
  - marketing and design.
- You need a strong leader with highly developed communication skills, diplomacy, persuasiveness and determination.
- They need to be a good negotiator, a good networker, with the ability and energy to be a beacon for others to follow.
- They need to act and think differently – if you need a chief customer officer it is because the company needs to rethink how it operates in relation to its customers, not do more of the same.
- Above all they need to see things from both the commercial and the customer's point of view, balancing those drivers to spot the opportunities that others may miss.

What are the main goals and activities for the customer experience lead?

The customer experience lead has four main goals:

- To increase revenue – by attracting and retaining more valuable customers and getting them to stay longer and spend more and by doing more of what works and less of what does not work for customers – this can provide a commercial component to the role even if there is no direct line authority.
- To bring balance to decision making – by focusing on customer value rather than traditional revenue and cost containment considerations.

- To grow customer equity – by managing customers as an important business asset.
- To drive and lead organisational change – by using customer insights to reveal the priority activities.

The main activities of the customer experience lead to deliver against these goals are:

- to take overall responsibility for leading the design of the customer experience and to guide others in this;
- encourage development initiatives and get the buy-in and resources from across the organisation (the CCO will not have direct responsibilities but will champion, guide and lead);
- encourage all internal divisions, partners, third-party agencies to each embrace the joint importance of the customer experience;
- identify and exploit best practice from inside and outside;
- encourage sharing, learning, feedback and continuous improvement;
- ensure that all customer-focused internal and external communications are developed with a clear understanding of the internal and external audience;
- champion deployment of customer- and employee-related measures that provide lead indicators for better forecasting and targeted actions;
- work closely with the HR team to connect the customer and employee propositions.

How do we make the customer experience lead successful?

There is a range of ways in which the lead can expect to be successful, but key will be the quick and positive engagement of the maximum number of people throughout the company. Some examples of tactical activity to deliver include:

- ensure that the CCO or Senior Vice President has a support team from day one;
- provide executive authority through the CEO or most senior executive director including joint communications;
- locate 'beacons' who will act as the first stage catalysts inside functions – managers who have a like view;

- introduce a CEO-endorsed secondment programme to the customer experience lead team making it 'the place to advance your career', so attracting the top talent;
- seek to add value early, provide support and assistance linked to commercial targets;
- focus hard on understanding current capabilities internally;
- focus early on understanding what customers value most and least today;
- generate high-profile, quick-win opportunities to stimulate interest and support;
- provide frameworks that help colleagues to deliver quickly on customer-related activity;
- push for a balanced scorecard and don't be afraid to take on financial targets;
- run 'sheep dip' learning sessions to get a quick increase in awareness.

Key focus areas for the new customer experience lead

Organisationally to develop and secure employee engagement by:

- defining key customer-related attributes for frontline staff;
- ensuring that staff know how important they are to delivering the brand promise and what their own contribution is – provide a feedback mechanism so staff know how to improve;
- empowering staff to be confident to do the right thing for customers.

Delivering a step change in the recruitment and development of frontline staff by:

- recruiting and developing frontline staff according to their service-oriented personality – technical and industry knowledge can be learnt;
- using existing staff to recruit the 'right people' – helps to build communities and reduce staff turnover;
- putting in place motivation and incentives to encourage the right behaviours – this can be team or individual – rewards should be based on outcomes rather than outputs;

- ensuring that senior managers demonstrate commitment to customer care, through leadership, performance management and active involvement with customers.

Ensuring that the service and product proposition matches customers' (and prospects') wants and needs by:

- developing a customer segmentation framework, based on customer-type attributes (life cycle, demographics, interests, etc.) and based on customer value, according to a decile split of value;
- using segmentation to tailor appropriate personalised service offerings through the development of customer personas to humanise the work of a segment team;
- focusing acquisition, retention and loyalty strategies on value-based segmentation;
- developing a structured approach to gathering customer (and employee) feedback and use to improve – customer panels have been shown to work well;
- asking customers 'what is the single thing we could do to improve?'

Ensuring that the experience compares favourably with that of other providers that customers deal with by:

- using customers and staff to provide feedback;
- undertaking research and using the knowledge to drive improvement.

Ensuring that the delivery of the customer experience matches the strategy and brand promise by:

- researching key service stages (welcoming, getting to know, upgrade, problem resolution, etc.) by mapping the customer journey;
- articulating the 'service personality' and making it easy for staff to know how to bring this to life.

Maximising existing knowledge and good practice by:

- developing a 'resource centre' to gather and spread best practice in customer care;

- rewarding best practice behaviour and using inspirational staff to help develop colleagues;
- ensuring that the customer experience delivers value for customers and business by segmenting the customer experience according to different customer preferences and drivers of loyalty.

Facilitating business change and business alignment by developing a focused customer-based strategy by:

- testing new initiatives against how well they contribute to this strategy;
- developing strategies for customer retention and development (cross-sell and upsell) based on a value-based segmentation strategy;
- getting to grips with ALL the committees and forums that either claim to be there for the customer or don't have a customer in them, in order to bring clarity and connectivity to the different groups.

Developing an understanding of what is working and the impact on business performance by:

- focusing measures on customer-based outcomes and outputs, rather than on operational inputs and processes;
- encouraging a continuous improvement and feedback loop by developing action plans from satisfaction, NPS and other survey results;
- putting in place channel measures to understand which channels perform best and most effectively;
- using 360° periodic assessments to check what is working and what needs to improve.

These actions will provide a powerful indicator, linking customer- and employee-related actions to increased commitment and improved business results.

Things to think about

To create the best opportunity to succeed in improving your customer experience and raise the profile of the customer in the development and deployment of your business strategy, take the low-key approach. Allow the successes to create the fuel for further work. Once you have some strong messages around the customer experience successes you can begin to raise the volume level internally and externally.

Aim to raise the profile of the experience to parity with the other key strategic drivers and fund and resource it to create the conditions to deliver success.

I have often used the analogy that gaining success in terms of the customer experience is like pushing a bus up a hill: in the early stages it is very hard work. Once the bus reaches the top of the hill and people see the business and personal benefits of engagement, you are hanging on trying to slow the bus down as it heads off on the downhill slope.

You must recognise the capability gaps in the company: whether at the senior level where they need support to drive confidence to contribute, down to the delivery teams where they need to think differently. Build in training and support at all levels to underwrite the success.

If you create a customer experience function ensure that it is supported and nurtured to avoid the risk of a cultural backlash.

This is about equipping teams and individuals to think like customers, think differently and challenge the status quo, and to influence the resulting customer experiences.

What did you think of this book?

We're really keen to hear from you about this book, so that we can make our publishing even better.

Please log on to the following website and leave us your feedback.

It will only take a few minutes and your thoughts are invaluable to us.

www.pearsoned.co.uk/bookfeedback

Index